AN ELFORD CHILDHOOD

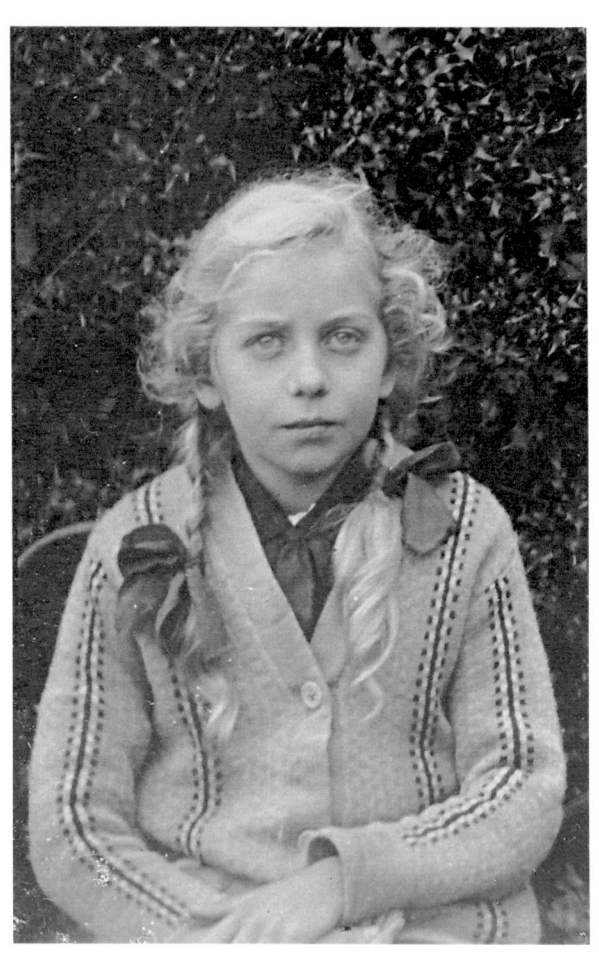

Doris Buttery, born 1920
Photograph c1930

AN ELFORD CHILDHOOD

Growing up in a Staffordshire Village 1920-1933

DORIS BUTTERY

UMBRIA PRESS

First published in 2022

Copyright ©Ann Nibbs 2022

The moral right of the editor has been asserted. All rights reserved. Without limiting the rights under copyright reserved above, no part of this publication may be reproduced, stored or introduced into a retrieval system, or transmitted, in any form or by any means (electronic, mechanical, photocopying, recording or otherwise) without the prior written permission of the copyright owner.

Published by Umbria Press
SW15 5DP
www.umbriapress.co.uk

Printed in Poland by Totem
www.totem.com.pl

ISBN: 978-1-910074-41-1

In Loving Memory
Doris May Buttery
23rd October 1920 – 13th March 2018

Contents

Introduction	vii

PART ONE: Village Life

Village Life	1
Sundays	10
Holidays	16
Enter – A Cat	21
Railway Folk and Other Occupations	26
The Strong Arm of the Law	29
More Local Characters	31
Newcomers and Gardens	38
The Village School	43
Elford Hall and the Last Squire	53
The Village Hall	58
St Peter's Church	63
Editor's Note	71

PART TWO: A Tale of Two Brothers

Introduction	75
Bill	77
Frank	93

Editor's Note	98
Editor's Afterword	99
Acknowledgements	102
Elford 2021	103

Introduction

My mother, Doris May Buttery (1920-2018) was the third and last of the children of Elizabeth (1883-1970 née Hinks), known as Lizzie, and John Thomas Buttery (1886-1965) known as Jack. Her brothers were William (Bill – 1909-1990), and George Frank (Frank – 1913-1970).

Mum wrote the following account of her childhood memories in several stages, probably commencing sometime in the mid to late 1960s and into the 1970s. (Please bear that in mind when reading: some of the phrases she uses are not regarded as politically correct in the twenty-first century). At the time she was writing, at least some of the people she mentions were still alive so, in case it might be published, she decided to change their names, and indeed the names of the village of Elford (which she called Tamford) and Tamworth (renamed Wigworth), along with a number of others. Fortunately, she left a key, listing the pseudonyms and real identities – at least of some of them. Thanks to the diligence of Greg Watkins, a local historian living in Elford today, I have now discovered the identities of a few more of the characters who play small, but nevertheless significant, roles in Mum's story and have dragged them out from behind their fictitious names. I am left unsure of whether Mr Day is his real name (perhaps it was Mr Knight? such was the not-so-subtle nature of Mum's subterfuge!) Inevitably, owing to the passage of time, I am not sure of some of the others either and they too will appear here under her allotted pseudonyms.

In editing, I have done little to alter her own words, merely added some punctuation now and again, and removed some instances of repetition.

Here then is her account of life in a small Midlands village a century ago – a world far removed from the one in which we all now live.

Ann Nibbs, Editor,
Southport, 2021

PART ONE
Village Life

Village Life

My father was demobilized in Spring 1919 with a bounty of £20 and no job. He was too proud to seek any kind of national assistance so he, my mother and two brothers lived on their savings whilst Dad cycled all over the Midlands looking for work. This he eventually obtained in the summer of 1919 when the advertisers were so impressed that he had bicycled nearly forty miles for an interview, they decided he really needed the job. Of course, it wasn't what he had been used to, but he was thankful to get it, especially as there was a rent-free house going with it.

He and Mother and the boys could not move in right away, however, as the existing occupant was expecting a baby and had been guaranteed the tenancy until after the birth. Dad obtained lodgings, first of all in Harlaston (a village two miles from Elford) and, after a few weeks, he moved in with a childless couple in Elford which was most convenient as he was, at that time, working there. Soon, his new employers acquired an ex-Army lorry and Dad was able to start the job for which he had been engaged, which was to deliver cattle feed from a warehouse in Tamworth to all the farms in the district. Some corn was ground at the water mill which belonged to Dad's employers and stood beside the river opposite our house in Elford.

A year after the rest of the family took up residence in Elford, I was born on 23rd October, 1920.

I suppose by modern standards we had very little, but

we didn't feel deprived in any way. In front of our house was a water pump which we shared with our next-door neighbours. Each morning Dad would fill up two large buckets with water from the pump. These buckets were kept carefully covered and stood on a small table in the kitchen. Beside them stood a jug, used to ladle water from the buckets into kettles. We had no water laid on in the house at all. Not many people in the village did.

The lavatory was across the yard and was of the bucket type which had to be emptied frequently into a hole Dad had dug in the garden. The council houses up the road had water closets, but the tenants had to carry water in a bucket to flush theirs.

Our weekly baths were taken in a big, galvanized bath in the back kitchen with water heated in the washing boiler. The bath was placed in the corner beside the boiler, and very cosy it was too, especially in winter. Soft rainwater was collected for the purpose in two huge storage tanks in the back yard and an assortment of butts. In an arid summer, when these ran dry, Dad and the boys (my elder brothers Bill and Frank) carried water from the river. I cannot remember this happening very often, but neither do I remember anyone complaining when it did.

There was, of course no electricity. We had oil lamps downstairs and candles in the bedrooms. Anyone wanting to visit the lavatory after dark had to take a hurricane lamp with them. On cold winter evenings bedrooms were made cosy with the lighting of a Valor heating stove, and each person had a hot brick, wrapped in flannel, to put in their feather bed. You had to be careful not to put your foot on the safety pin which secured the wrapping (ouch!).

l-r Bill (aka Billy), Frank, Lizzie, Jack and Doris outside their home in Elford, 1930 (you can just see a few of Jack's much-prized roses to the left of the photograph)

The bricks used to be placed in the oven immediately after tea and, with the huge fires which cheered our winter evenings, they became very hot indeed.

We never suffered any shortage of fuel. A ton of coal was delivered each September and tipped (loose) by our front gate. We all lent a hand in the carrying of it into the coalhouse.

Under the apple tree in the back garden, we had a 'stick-nick'. These were stacked tree trunks ready for sawing into logs and smaller pieces which were chopped to make kindling. Quite near our house was a small wood and we often collected firewood there. On the roadside opposite were several elms and on many a windy night Dad was awakened by a motorist requesting help to move a fallen tree off the road. All of these ultimately found their way into our fire.

We were self-sufficient as far as fruit and vegetables went. In addition to the large garden belonging to the house, Dad rented some tithe land across the road which ran along the back of our house. There he grew potatoes and turnips. A large part of our garden was taken up with a poultry run. Mother kept white wyandottes and made a few shillings selling eggs to people from the town. She had regular customers and they were never let down. If the hens were off laying, we were the ones who did without eggs. Never the customers.

Each spring, Dad would buy a hatch of day-old chicks and the same thing always happened. As soon as he brought them home, Mother and I would spread newspaper on the kitchen floor, open the box and lift out the yellow chirruping, fluffy balls. Mother would scatter a little chick food and we would drool over these delightful little babies. Dad would scold us for picking them up and stroking them, but he knew it was useless because neither Mother nor I could resist them. Soon he would come and collect them and put them in a coop with a broody hen who would cluck with delight as they nestled beneath her. I always marvelled that never once did any of our hens squash a chick.

Next day the door of the coop would be opened, and the chicks and their foster mother would be allowed into the chicken run. My brother Frank and I spent many happy hours digging up worms for them and how we laughed to see a chick at either end of a worm disputing ownership. I'm afraid we never gave a thought to the poor worm.

We also kept a pig in a sty in the adjoining meadow. This land belonged to Dad's employers, and they allowed him to make use of the buildings on it. Frank and I were given the task of gathering comfrey which grew wild along the side of the road and is highly nutritious for pigs.

On the day our pig was to be slaughtered I used to be sent off earlier than usual to school. The pig bench would already be set out in the back yard and the water in the copper was boiling in readiness. As I went through the gate, Mr Wilson, the pig killer, and Dad would be going through the meadow to fetch the pig. By the time I got home again, everything would be cleaned away and the two halves of the animal hung suspended from the hooks on the centre beam in the kitchen. But, on one never-to-be-forgotten day, Mother had to go into the nearby town of Tamworth on some urgent errand. There were few trains a day from our little station, so she left Mr Wilson to lock up. I had known she would not be in when I returned home from school, but on such occasions, I knew the back-door key would be on a ledge in the lavatory so I could let myself in. It didn't happen very often, and, in any case, Mother was always home within half an hour of my arrival.

On that particular day, I opened the back door and there immediately facing me was the pig on its hooks with a bowl below to catch the drips. I had seen this sight many times, but I had never actually been alone in the house with a dead pig, so I carefully closed and re-locked the door, replaced the key in its hiding place and went to call on Miss Case who lived next door. Frank was at college so when mother returned and found I was not at home she guessed where I must be. She herself had been taken aback by the sight which greeted her when she opened the door. It was definitely not what she had instructed.

I would have been about seven or eight years old at the time, but Miss Case told Mother I had not mentioned being frightened at all. After all these years, I cannot remember whether I was or not, but it clearly made some impression on me, or I wouldn't remember it so vividly all these years later. Mother, of course, was very concerned, but it was alright now she was home.

Nowadays people would be horrified at the idea of a seven-year-old letting themselves into an empty house where there was an open fire, even though it was well guarded. In those days however, we were so well-drilled in home safety, almost from birth, that accidents were a rarity. In fact, I do not recall a single incident of burning or scalding in our village. It would never have occurred to any of us to play with matches which were, in any case, kept well out of reach. Nor would we have dreamed of interfering with the fire. Only older children were allowed to 'make it up'. Younger ones steered well clear.

In the house next to ours lived Mr Day, the manager of the mill. Miss Case was his live-in housekeeper. Mr Day was a soldierly looking man with silvery hair and a military moustache. He was in his late fifties and Miss Case would be fortyish. She was, in my mother's opinion, not a very good housekeeper as she tended to be a bit slapdash in her methods, but she evidently looked after Mr Day well enough. Before she arrived on the scene, his housekeeper had been a Miss Graham who had been with him for nearly thirty years. It was after she died of cancer that Miss Case came to keep house for him.

I liked Mr Day a lot and often used to go round and see him. He was always kind and seemed to have time to listen and talk to me.

We were one of the first households in the village to own a wireless set, which my brother Bill had built from a blueprint. Dad told me I was not to tell anyone we had one, so I promptly told Mr Day next time I saw him. I was perhaps around four years old at the time.

'I hear you've got a wireless set,' Mr Day said to Dad the next time he saw him.

'Now who told you that?' asked Dad.

'The little girl told me.'

'Oh,' replied Dad. 'Well, yes, we have. I bought the licence today.'

I heard this exchange so was quite surprised when Dad asked, 'Why did you tell Mr Day about the wireless when I said you were not to tell anyone?'

'I didn't think you meant I couldn't tell Mr Day,' I replied.

'Well, when I say you're not to tell anyone that includes Mr Day in future.'

Of course, I realize now that it was on account of the licence that I was supposed to keep quiet. In those days, before television, if you had a wireless you must buy a licence and that was an expense my parents could well have done without.

One morning, when I was around eight years old, we were awakened by Miss Case hammering on our door.

Dad opened the door.

Her voice trembled. 'Please can you come? I can't rouse Mr Day. I'm sure he's dead.'

Dad hurried next door, saying he didn't suppose Mr Day was dead at all, but he was soon back to get properly dressed to go across to the Mill to telephone for a doctor.

'Not that it's much use,' he remarked as he left the house.

The doctor came on his motor bike and confirmed our old friend had indeed passed away. Miss Case was quite overcome by the suddenness, as were we all.

Dad took on the responsibility of informing Mr Day's cousins, who lived some distance away, and they arrived promptly to make arrangements for the funeral.

Now, what they did not know, but both Dad and Miss Case did, was that for many years Mr Day and Miss Graham had enjoyed an intimate relationship. After pondering on this for a while, Dad went round to see the relative, along with Miss Case.

'Has anyone,' he asked, 'informed Miss Pearl Day?'

'Miss Pearl Day?' came the chorus of amazement. 'Who on earth is she?'

'Pearl is Mr Day's daughter,' Dad replied.

They turned to Miss Case.

'Did you know of this?' One of them asked.

'Oh yes,' she nodded. 'Miss Pearl has stayed here several times.'

Then, of course, confusion reigned because no one knew her address. Both Dad and Miss Case knew she lived in Rugby but that was all.

Fortunately, the next day, a letter arrived for Mr Day, and Miss Case recognized the handwriting. She took it to Dad who opened it, made sure it was from Pearl and sent off a telegram.

Pearl arrived with her fiancé late that evening. She was a charming young woman and as soon as the cousins saw her, they knew her parentage could not be disputed. She was so much like her father in looks and mannerisms. Naturally, it wasn't until much later in my life that I learned all this. In those days, such things were never discussed in front of children.

I do remember, however, that Pearl's fiancé came rushing into our house saying, 'I can't believe it. I just can't believe it,' and Dad following him in and telling him to pull himself together and think of Pearl.

After he had gone, I remember Dad saying that the young man wasn't half good enough for Pearl.

When I asked Mother about this many years later, she told me that Pearl's fiancé had been shocked to discover she was illegitimate. Mother said she wondered if they'd ever married because she thought he was the sort of man who would let such a thing prey on his mind.

Sundays

Sunday was always a day of rest in our house. No unnecessary work was ever done. We children attended church in the morning. In the afternoon, Sunday School took place in the village school, for children between the ages of four and seven, whilst the older children went to church for catechism with the rector.

On a Sunday evening, Mother, Dad and I either went to church or, if the weather was especially pleasant, went for a long walk. There were some lovely walks around Elford and, of course, comparatively little motor traffic to spoil the peace of the countryside.

Sometimes we would walk along Green Lane, which was rather like a bridle path, running from the road at the back of our house right round onto the main Tamworth Road. It was a fascinating place to wander along. At one point, where the path widened, a pond provided the perfect spot for us children to take our nets to fish for minnows, which we put into jam jars. But not on Sundays, of course. These tiny fish never lived long after we got them home and I couldn't understand why I was not allowed to keep them in a soft water tank!

The countryside provided endless bounty. Blackberry briars came richly laden with berries in late summer. The wildflowers were, of course, a joy, and all kinds of birds built their nests in the hedgerows and bushes. We delighted in finding that the thrush, yellowhammer, blackbird, and more had returned to the same spot year after year.

Another favourite walk took us across the fields to Harlaston. This route involved crossing a railway line, so we took great care after climbing the stile. We mounted the steps up the embankment, stopped to look both ways along the line and to listen carefully. The path across the fields had been a right of way long before the railways came, so it had to be preserved and was, in fact, well used. In all the years we lived in Elford, there was never an accident – another example of discipline and good training. No child would have dreamed of loitering whilst crossing the line, let alone playing there.*

I travelled along that railway line a year or two ago*. It is now electrified and the stiles on either side of the line have disappeared. Possibly some other arrangement has been made for people wishing to walk over the fields, but more probably the right of way lapsed as more and more people acquired cars.

The walk from the railway line was entirely over grazing land and brought us out into the centre of the village of Harlaston. One Sunday we set out that way, but our progress was barred by notices warning of an outbreak of Foot and Mouth Disease. We went by the road and, as we came alongside the meadows, dead cattle were being dragged into a huge pit, dug for the purpose. It is a sight I will never forget, and I think, even now, some townsfolk do not fully appreciate the horror of that devastating disease. It is not only the loss of valuable beasts but the effect on a farmer of seeing, what is probably, their life's work disappearing in a few short hours. That particular farmer lost an entire pedigree dairy herd.

On arrival in Harlaston, we would usually call on Mrs

Inkberrow, the lady with whom Dad had lodged briefly when he first joined his present employers. She was a silvery-haired lady and always made us very welcome.

Then we would sometimes cross the road to the White Lion where we would sit at a table in the garden. Mother and I would enjoy a glass of refreshing lemonade whilst Dad had a pint of beer. He would usually buy a small packet of biscuits for me and that was a real treat, especially if they were custard creams, because we only ever had Marie or Arrowroot biscuits at home. After our little rest for refreshment, we would wend our way homewards, going by the road for a change of scenery.

Once home, Mother would bustle about, cutting a slice of bread on which she thickly spread dripping from the Sunday joint. This was my Sunday supper, washed down with a cup of milk. I still enjoy bread and dripping, and toast and dripping is tasty too.

If Mother was feeling a little less energetic, our Sunday night walk would take us through the wood near our home. We made our way along the bottom path where, in places, there was a sheer drop to the river. I was not supposed to venture along here on my own. I did, of course, but never when heavy rain had made the going treacherous, and I always used tree roots as handrails while carefully picking my way along, but I don't remember ever walking the entire length of the bottom path alone until I was about eleven years old.

When we reached the end of the wood, we returned along the safer top path. This wood was carpeted with bluebells in spring, and, on a bank between the wood and the road, sweetly scented wild violets grew in profusion.

Approaching Elford early 1930s

One had to search for them amongst the fallen leaves, but the effort was well worthwhile.

There was one other favourite walk of ours. We crossed the ancient river bridge along a narrow winding lane through the hamlet of Fisherwick, until we came to a canal. We usually went this way when blackberries were in season because the canal-side banks were covered with brambles. In no time at all, our baskets would be filled with large, juicy berries. Because it was Sunday, we always took our walks wearing our best clothes, so had to be particularly careful not to get stains on them. Despite our best efforts, we often found tell-tale purple marks somewhere when we got home.

On summer Sundays, most of the little girls in the village wore white dresses and yellow straw hats, secured on our heads by narrow elastic under our chins. Gloves were essential. As we grew older, we were allowed to wear pastel colours. Our clothes were usually home-made but, if we were lucky enough to have a 'bought' dress, we really felt like 'somebody'. Mother used to make my light summer coats, and I hated the colour, which was always fawn.

Our winter Sunday best was more varied. I can remember having a pink coat and hat trimmed with fur, but quite often, my winter coat was navy blue frieze cloth, with a black velour hat. My dress would be either woollen - hand-knitted - or blue serge with a silk collar. I once had a Saxe-blue sunray-pleated skirt and matching woollen jumper. A lot of the girls wore dresses of golden-brown velveteen, and I was very envious, but Mother thought it too impractical. I had to have something which could be washed!

Mother was very strict on Sunday observance. No games of any kind were allowed, whether they were ball games or card games. Even ludo and draughts were forbidden. When I was six, Mother, Frank and I went for a holiday to Rhyl – my first visit to the seaside – but I was not allowed to build sandcastles until the Monday as we had arrived too late on the Saturday for playing on the beach. I felt very badly used.

Even after we were all grown up and married, none of us would have dared to suggest playing cards on a Sunday, nor would I or my sisters-in-law have brought out our knitting. The only sewing allowed was in emergency, such as replacement of a button.

It sounds ridiculous now, and yet perhaps it wasn't so silly. It gave us all time to read, and write letters, or just relax generally. Not a bad thing, after all, especially after a hard week's work.

Holidays

Not many people in the village were able to go away for an annual holiday unless they went to stay with relatives. The families of some of the railwaymen managed an occasional trip to Blackpool, travelling on their free passes.

As I mentioned earlier, we went to Rhyl for a week when I was six. As there was livestock to be looked after, Mother and Dad could never go away together at the same time, so that was why Mother alone accompanied Frank and me on that holiday. Our usual holiday comprised of a couple of weeks with my grandfather in Shropshire. He was Mother's father, a farm bailiff, who owned the house he lived in along with the two meadows adjoining it. Like the rest of that village (Tibberton), it had once been part of the estate of the Dukes of Sutherland. When the estate was being sold, in the early part of the twentieth century*, tenants were given the opportunity of buying the house in which they lived. Grandfather's house had been tenanted by Grandmother's family for longer than anyone could remember and, although she was dead by then, Grandfather decided to buy it and was able to borrow sufficient money to enable him to do so.

My widowed aunt, Mother's eldest sister, kept house for him. Auntie Sallie had lost her husband in the 1918 'flu pandemic when their youngest child Kathleen was a week old. The same pandemic had also carried off Mother's youngest sister, Auntie Flo, who was keeping house for

Grandfather at the time, so it seemed sensible for Auntie Sallie, her sons, Wally and Jack, and baby Kathleen to move in with Grandfather.

The boys were both at school and, as soon as they were old enough to leave, they went to live in Birmingham with their father's brother who found them work on the railway. Kathleen, however, stayed on with her mother, and I enjoyed having her to play with when we went there to stay. She was a couple of years older than me, but we shared the same interests, and I could join in any activities in which she and her friends were involved.

Unlike ours in Elford, milk was not delivered to Grandfather's house, so Kathleen had to collect it every morning and night from the farm. This was a novelty to me as I went with her. But I suspect that would have soon worn off if I had to do it regularly in all weathers and all seasons.

Doris on her bicycle, Elford c.1930-1932

Like us, Grandfather kept pigs in a sty at the top of his extensive garden, and his privy adjoined the pigsty. This privy comprised of two comfortable round holes in a wooden seat of an earth closet. Kathleen and I used to sit side by side on a warm summer day and watch men at work in the fields or read one of the many copies of *The Family Journal* which used to accumulate there.

Grandfather also had a couple of cowsheds, along with a third in the far meadow. Fruit trees abounded – pears, apples (both cooking and dessert), damsons and plums. The sweetest plum was a pale, yellow round 'sugar' plum – or at least that's what everyone called it. The tree was ancient, and the crop diminished over the years, but the flavour remained constant. Juicy and so sweet that hardly any sugar was needed when they were cooked. That tree stood conveniently (for Kathleen and me) right beside the cow shelter in the far meadow. We used to climb up onto the roof and sit there, gorging ourselves. If the plums were out of reach, we would shake the tree and eat the fallen fruit. We deserved to be made ill but, strangely, never were. At least, not as a result of eating 'sugar' plums.

One day we had just given the tree a vigorous shaking when we saw Mother coming through the meadow with a basket on her arm, headed straight for our tree. We sat silently on the cow shelter roof until she had picked up a basketful and returned to the house. We had been ticked off on several occasions for climbing onto that roof so we hoped our presence would go unnoticed. We were lucky, but how hard it was to keep silent as we ate our pudding that day, and Mother said, 'I was really surprised at the number of plums on the ground today. After all, it isn't as if we've had any winds.'

Auntie Sallie did a lot of work for the village. She was secretary of the Women's Institute, a member of the Parochial Church Council (as was Grandfather) and also involved with organising dances and whist drives held at the Institute. She was a born organiser with a will of iron. As a result, there were occasional clashes between her and Mother, who also liked to have her own way and, like many tiny people, knew how to get it. On the whole, however, those Shropshire country holidays were happy times, and there were always tears when the time came for Kathleen and me to part.

Doris, aged 11, in fancy dress outside the cottage in Elford, Jan 1st 1932

Enter – A Cat

As a small child, I was terrified of fur and caused my parents acute embarrassment by screaming if anyone wearing it came anywhere near me. This happened with alarming frequency. After all, it was the 1920s when practically every woman had some scrap of fur which would duly emerge from mothballs every Sunday to be worn in church.

Dad and Mother decided the only solution was a cat* and duly obtained a small tortoiseshell kitten. This turned out to be a shrewd move as I became besotted with her and was soon pushing the long-suffering animal around in my doll's pram. She was called Fluff and seemed to know why she had come to live with us, for she even allowed me to dress her in my doll's bonnet and coat. Then she would obligingly go to sleep with her head on the pram pillow. She was much more interesting than an inanimate rag doll and I was never again afraid of fur.

Fluff grew up of course, and in due time presented us with a litter of kittens, several of which bore strong resemblance to Sooty, the tomcat who lived with Mr Day next door.

All the kittens went to good homes, and Fluff became my playmate again for a time. She had, however, developed a liking for hunting rabbits in the corn field behind our house. The farmer there was a short-tempered man, and Dad had crossed swords with him on several occasions when shots from the farmer's gun had seemed a bit wild.

There were hundreds of rabbits about, so I cannot think that the odd one caught by a cat can have represented such a great financial loss to him, but he saw red whenever he saw a feline on his land. One lady in the village owned a beautiful Blue Persian, and this same farmer knocked on her door one afternoon to tell her that if she wanted her cat, it was lying by the hedge in one of his fields as he had seen it stalking a rabbit and had shot it. She was heartbroken, but he was merciless in his war on felines.

He had a fright one day though. It was on a summer Saturday afternoon, and I was playing on the lids of the soft water tanks. A shot rang out, followed by an immediate unearthly scream. I jumped down as Mr Day's black cat raced pell-mell down the back path, along our yard, and into the coal-shed. He was making a terrible noise exactly like a child in agony. Dad sent me indoors and, as he went to look for the tortured animal, the farmer came dashing into the yard, his face white as he asked, 'Where's your little girl? Have I hit her?'

Dad was blunt. 'No, you haven't, but don't worry, you will if you keep trying.'

'It was a cat after rabbits…' began the farmer as the dreadful noise from the coal-shed continued.

'Yes,' said Dad. 'It was a cat. Mr Day's cat. You might as well finish what you started and put the poor beast out of its misery. Then you can go and tell Mr Day.'

Poor Mr Day was terribly upset, and, after that, we kept Fluff in as much as possible, but cats cannot be so easily confined as dogs.

Our promiscuous cat had another litter, and this time Mother kept one kitten because she looked so much like

Fluff. It must have been a premonition because, when the kitten was weaned, Fluff suffered the same fate as poor Sooty, only we hoped it was quicker.

Fluff II was as affectionate as her mother and just as prolific. When she was three, she tired of having her babies taken from her right at the time they became interesting, so decided to do something about it. For two days, she went missing, and Mother was beginning to think she had met her end with a bullet from the farmer's gun when she reappeared. She had obviously had her kittens, but no one knew where. We searched all the likely and most of the unlikely places, without result.

For six weeks, Fluff appeared regularly morning and evening for her food but, although many hours were wasted in watching, none of us could track her to her nursery. When she saw us watching, she sat down to have a wash. As soon as you looked the other way for a second, she disappeared.

Mr Day made the discovery as he was digging his garden one evening. He thought he heard something high in his apple tree while he rested for a moment. He looked up, expecting to see a bird, and saw instead a tiny furry face.

Fluff was eating her supper, so Mr Day got his ladder and climbed up quietly to investigate. There, in a hollow in the centre of the tree, were three beautiful kittens. He left them and came to tell Mother. She and Frank hurried along there. Frank carefully removed each swearing, spitting ball of fur and handed it to Mother. Fluff was by this time aware of what was going on and stood beside Mother, mewing and calling to her babies.

Mother put them in her apron and, followed by an anxious Fluff, bore them into the house where she released them onto the kitchen floor. They immediately tottered unsteadily towards the darkest corner, despite Fluff's attempts at reassurance. They had been so restricted in the hollow tree that they were not very steady on their legs and kept toppling over. Frank came with a cardboard box in which he had put some newspaper, and, with some difficulty, we caught the frightened kittens and put them inside. Fluff jumped in beside them and managed to settle them down. The kittens were all beautifully marked tabbies and, after we had tamed them, we had no difficulty in finding them good homes.

Fluff II disappeared completely when she was about five years old. We never did find out what happened to her but suspected she had met the same fate as her mother. As Dad remarked, she was, at a distance, a bit rabbit-coloured herself so, if she had been shot, it could have been by mistake, although, of course, it would have made no difference to that cat-hating farmer if she had been purple!

Mother refused to have another cat. It was too upsetting when they met their end and, anyway, it was obvious that as long as we lived there, no cat would be safe from a bullet or a snare. In fact it was not until I was fifteen, and we had left Elford for Tamworth, that we had another cat. Another tortoiseshell. We called her Jo.

It was after Fluff II disappeared that we acquired a temporary pet of a different kind. Bill found a young owl by the roadside and brought it home. Its wing was damaged, probably by a passing car or by striking the telegraph wires.

He put it into an old hen coop and cared for it until one day when Mother removed the front bars and it was able to fly, rather feebly, to our apple tree. We left the coop in the same place so that it could return if it wished, and Mother left food and water handy. It hung around for another week or so, then flew right away.

Frank then got hold of some rabbits. Mother did not think very much of those, and they did not last long. Their appetites were insatiable, and Frank soon found they took up a lot of his time in keeping them clean. He took them to school, one by one, and gave them to other boys.

That was the end of our pet-keeping activities in Elford. We have never been a dog family but, from starting as an infant who hated fur, I developed into someone who is a fool over cats. I find them quite irresistible, possessed of so much character and intelligence. Whoever it was who said, 'Dogs look up to you, cats look down on you, but pigs is equal', knew what they were talking about, in my opinion. Every cat who has owned me has left me in no doubt that I am there for her convenience, whilst the pigs we used to keep could, on occasion, take on an almost human identity.

Railway Folk and Other Occupations

Although a good half of the menfolk of Elford were agricultural workers, the other half followed a wide variety of occupations. There were a number of railwaymen, most of whom were employed on maintenance of the permanent way, although as we boasted a tiny station, where eight trains stopped daily, we had a stationmaster, a porter and a signalman living in the village. The station was three-quarters of a mile from the centre, and the stationmaster—whose house was part of the station buildings—and his family took little or no part in village life. In fact, the whole family were, for some obscure reason, aloof from the rest of us, and appeared to consider the social life of Elford beneath them. At least, that was the impression they gave, but I have since wondered if it was rather that they could not afford to join in.

The son, who was a little older than my brother Frank, went to the same Business School (Lawrence's College) in Birmingham as he did but whereas Frank went on there from the village school at fourteen, Harry had been there from the age of ten. There were three daughters and the elder two were sent to Tamworth High School at eleven years of age. The younger girl, who was thought to be rather 'delicate', remained at the village school because her parents thought her health was so uncertain that she would probably be unable to earn her own living. They felt that sending her to the High School would be a waste of money. On point of fact, when the war came in 1939, she obtained a job in a bank and did well there.

The stationmaster's wife must have led a rather lonely and dreary sort of life. The only people she met outside the family were railway passengers when she went to Tamworth to do her shopping. The stationmaster was always pleasantly civil to the travelling public, but I never saw him in any clothes other than his uniform. I did not know Mildred, the elder daughter, because she was already at Tamworth High when I started at the village school and by the time I went to the High School, she had already left. An older friend, who remembered her from High School days, told me that she was a frightful snob, but viewing the situation from this distance of time, I wonder if that too was part of a defence mechanism. On the few occasions when I did see her, she always appeared to be smartly dressed but it could be that there was no money to spare for extra-mural activities, so she pretended to be bored by them.

The second daughter, Evelyn, was a down-to-earth sort of person, quiet and friendly at school, but she too took no active part in anything that involved extra money.

The difference between Mildred and Evelyn seems to have been that Evelyn showed interest, but did not become involved, except perhaps to help with the sewing of costumes for a school play or listen to members of the cast rehearsing their lines

Some of the railwaymen lived in farm cottages for which they paid a small rent. In addition, their wives were expected to mend sacks and help with potato picking. The women were not paid for mending sacks, but they were not in a position to refuse. If they did, the farmer would threaten them with eviction.

I remember Mother telling Dad about this in scandalized tones. A woman used to come to help with the washing every Monday. This was a big, heavy job in those pre-washing machine days and Mother's health was such that she was not able to do it by herself. This one Monday, the woman, who was married to a railway linesman, told Mother that she had a huge pile of sacks to mend when she got home that day. This was a regular routine. The farmer would deliver the sacks one day and they had to be mended and ready for collection three days later. Both my parents were country folk, but this was something new to them and they disapproved very strongly of such exploitation.

The Strong Arm of the Law

Elford shared its village 'bobby' with the nearby village of Harlaston. There cannot have been very much for him to do because I don't remember any crimes more serious than 'scrumping' or riding a bike without a light. The latter was an all-too common offence. In those days most bicycles were equipped with acetylene lamps, and a thoroughgoing nuisance they were too. A gust of wind, or a pothole in the road, and out would go the light.

It became quite a regular thing on a Saturday night for the village constable from Wigginton to lie in wait for the young folk cycling back after visiting the cinema in Tamworth. If he missed any of the no-light brigade, there was always a chance they'd be caught a couple of miles further on by the representative of the law in Elford. The policemen were on bikes too though, so it was a case of who could pedal fastest. Both my brothers were caught on different occasions and hauled up before Tamworth Magistrates. In each case they were let off with a small fine, which was nothing compared to the ticking-off they received from Dad.

The policemen in those days had to be present at the dipping of sheep, and to see that the pub closed on time, but I wonder if the latter was such a chore. During the Second World War, I visited that same pub, in company with a crowd of other servicemen and girls. It was well past closing time but one of our party had been there before. He knocked several times on the back door which was soon opened. We all sidled into the kitchen, and there, seated at the table, jacket undone, was the local arm of the law. We were all made most welcome and no one saw any need for us to leave until it became quite clear that, if we were to meet the deadline of being back in Barracks by 23:59 hours, we had better be on our way. I am certainly not suggesting country policemen are lax – far from it – but I think they had a knack of building up confidence amongst the community they served and protected. We knew they were there to enforce the law, but they were by no means the pompous nitwits projected in some farces of the period.

More Local Characters

We had one 'professionally unemployed' man in the village. There were none of the present-day social security benefits, although I suppose he must have had some 'dole' money. He was called Sam and he lived with his mother. From time-to-time Sam would be found work road-mending or some other kind of labouring job, but after a couple of weeks he would be sacked. No one knew how he and his mother lived, but she always looked neat and tidy. I suppose he managed to scrounge a few shillings here and there.

He habitually wore a dark purple overcoat fastened back at the rear with safety pins to keep it clear of his bicycle wheels, and a dark-coloured cap along with a white muffler around his neck, and bicycle clips. Every Friday, he would cycle into Tamworth to 'sign on', returning during the afternoon. He was between thirty and forty years of age and had been in the Army during the First World War. After demobilization, he seemed to have decided that, henceforth, work was not for him. People ridiculed him and felt sorry for his mother. It must have been a very drab and dreary sort of life for both of them. But no one seemed to know what his mother thought about it because she kept herself to herself.

The postmistress, on the other hand, was a forbidding, elderly woman called Miss Sharp. She was tall, with iron grey hair scraped back into a bun, and gold-rimmed pince-nez perched on her – rather pointed – nose. She ran the

Post Office with the utmost efficiency and earned everyone's respect. In those days of the late 1920s, the only telephones in the village were at the Hall, the Mill and the Post Office, so many a time a child who happened to be lurking around the Post Office would be sent scampering off by Miss Sharp to tell Mr So-and-so he was wanted on the telephone. I performed this service several times and felt very important about it too. After all, it is not often than an eight-year-old can send an entire farming household running in different directions, looking for a farmer who is wanted on a telephone about a quarter of a mile away. I think the caller must have been quite desperate to speak to whoever they were calling because they often had to wait twenty minutes.

In those days the post was so completely reliable that, for three halfpence, a letter could be guaranteed to arrive next day anywhere in the country. Indeed, a letter posted in Birmingham before nine a.m. would be delivered during the evening of that same day in Southampton.

Miss Sharp was also the relief organist at church and played for funerals and, when required, for weekday weddings. I specify, 'when required' because only the better-off families bothered to have music for their wedding or, for that matter, for their funerals.

I was about ten years old when Miss Sharp died suddenly. She lived quite alone, so it was only when the Post Office van driver called to deliver the mail one morning and was unable to get a reply, that anyone realized something was wrong.

The postwoman who delivered the letters in the village came along, and, between them they managed to get inside. There they found Miss Sharp dead in a chair. This caused a great 'to-do' in the village, and the Post Office remained closed all that day.

Next day, someone came out from Tamworth to take care of the Post Office until a new postmaster and postmistress could be appointed. Meanwhile, relatives of the dead woman gathered on the scene. There was no one particularly close, but several cousins arrived and began a thorough search for a will. Everyone felt sure she had made one, but none of the solicitors in Tamworth had drawn one up for her. There were no close friends, but people who had known her for many years were confident she would have left clear instructions somewhere regarding the disposal of her property. She was, after all, the essence of organisation and orderliness.

Many weeks went by, and many hours were spent searching every nook and cranny. Books were shaken, chairs almost pulled apart, cushions ripped open, but no will was ever found. Eventually the relatives decided to abandon the search, and the house and contents were put up for auction.

The house was bought privately by the man and woman who had been appointed to run the Post Office and, when the contents were sold, the village had the time of its life. Mother went, along with almost every other woman in the village.

Miss Sharp had, it appeared, been unlucky in love, for there were trunks, boxes and baskets filled with brand new bed and table linen, towels, china, cutlery and, most intriguing of all, fine lawn nightdresses, petticoats, 'drawers' and chemises (six of each), all beautifully hand-stitched and trimmed with broderie anglaise or handmade lace. It was only when these treasure chests were revealed that some of the older residents recalled having heard of a broken romance when Miss Sharp moved to the village fifty years previously. Her father had been a prosperous coal merchant and he was delighted when his only daughter became engaged to the son of one of his oldest friends.

But, a month before the wedding, the prospective bridegroom departed and was next heard of in Australia whence he had gone with a clerk from his father's office whom he had married before leaving England. The shock caused Mr Sharp to have a heart attack from which he never recovered.

The linen and underwear had yellowed with age, but it was obvious that they were of the highest quality, while some of the sheets were still in their original parcels which contained the receipted bill. Many women sighed and clucked sympathetically as the various items came under the auctioneer's hammer. But the sighs turned to smiles and giggles when some of the underwear was held up for inspection.

※ ※ ※

There was only one Public House in the village and that was called *The Crown*. The landlord was Mr Rowe and, in addition to being a publican, he was a farmer of some standing, and he also had a coal lorry. There were four sons and three daughters, all of whom helped their parents one way or another. Milk had to be delivered before the younger children went to school and each child in turn learned how to handle a horse and float from a very early age. The milk was in churns and measured out into the customer's own jugs. In the winter, chilblains made this a punishing operation. Mother used to be most concerned when she saw the red and swollen fingers struggling painfully with the measures.

At weekends, poultry houses had to be cleaned out. This was a job undertaken by both boys and girls of the family. I particularly recall one of the girls – Rachel - complaining bitterly that she could never get her hands to look clean after mucking out the hen houses.

Grace and Mary, the elder daughters, helped their mother in the house and the dairy. Mrs Rowe made butter, some of which she sold to people in the village – including us. Grace was the oldest in the family and engaged to a neighbouring farmer. Next to her came Roger and then John. Roger used to be in charge of the coal delivery and, shortly after John became old enough to drive a motor vehicle, Mr Rowe inherited a sizeable sum of money which he used to buy two new lorries. These he used for collecting milk from farms round about, transporting it to a large dairy in Birmingham for bottling. Soon he had made enough money to buy a fourth lorry and he employed another driver. Thus began a flourishing road haulage business.

Mrs Rowe was a nice woman but inclined to look down her nose a little at some of the village girls, especially those who anticipated marriage. She had been heard to speak her mind forcibly on this subject one day at a meeting of the Mothers' Union so it was unfortunate that within a year, Roger, Grace and John all married rather more quickly than they had intended. The villagers remembered and wagged their heads as their tongues worked overtime, especially those mothers who had themselves been placed in a similar position. One or two even took a fiendish delight in offering sympathy.

❋ ❋ ❋

Every village was reckoned to have its 'village idiot' and Elford was no exception. I doubt if the unfortunate man was actually 'mentally deficient'. He was certainly harmless but had great difficulty with his speech and walked with queer jerking movements. The children used to run after him and call him names, and when he turned suddenly to face his tormentors, they would run away, shrieking, as he said, 'You mustn't laugh at me-ee.'

I was expressly forbidden to take part in this because my parents felt great sympathy for the poor man. No doubt nowadays he would have received proper diagnosis, professional help, education and training, but then he was treated as a freak. Every so often his mother would visit the school to complain about the children's behaviour, and things would go quiet for a while but then it would start again. He must have been about forty years old at that time, so his mother would be over sixty. I've often wondered how he fared when she died. He came of a large family so perhaps a kindly brother or sister gave him shelter.

Although times were hard, as children we were not made terribly aware of it. After all, no one in the village had much money and although some were obviously better off than others, it really depended on the size of the family. At any rate we, in our family, never knew hunger, nor were we ever cold for lack of warm clothing. We never had a lot of clothes and when I started at the High School and had to wear school uniform, that became my 'best' as well as my school wear. I had to change into older things when I arrived home each evening and, unless we were going somewhere special on a Saturday, I wore older clothes then as well. There was never any question of what came first and indeed, for many years and in many families, that was the rule. School uniform had to be worn, so any other clothing purchase came a very poor second.

Only once did Mother relent and it was I who later wished she hadn't. I begged and begged to be allowed to have a different coloured winter coat instead of the same old navy blue. I was about fourteen at the time and we had left Elford. Reluctantly, Mother bought me a light blue-grey coat. The following year, my school coat was so outgrown that there was no alternative to wearing the light-coloured coat for school. Although it was not strictly forbidden, any colour other than navy was viewed with disapproval and I felt so conspicuous and embarrassed. How I hated it! I vowed then that no child of mine would ever be in such a position.

Newcomers and Gardens

Many of the families in Elford had lived in the village for generations and there had been quite a lot of intermarriage.

There were however a few newcomers like us, and how quickly they were accepted depended on how ready they were to conform to the ways of the village and to participate in the various activities. On the whole most people fitted in well. There was something comfortable about knowing that a letter addressed to Mrs So-and-so, Elford, would be delivered because everyone knew everyone else and there was no need for a more detailed address. Most people did, of course, use their proper addresses but if they didn't, well – not to worry – the letter would arrive at its proper destination on time.

The only new houses built in the village during the 1920s were eight semi-detached council houses, set in a row, not far from our own cottage. In the first of these lived a Scottish family called Gordon. Mr Gordon, like our rector's brother-in-law, Mr Prince, had been a veterinary surgeon. Unfortunately, also like Mr Prince, he had become mentally unstable. When the Gordons first went to live there, he was already showing signs of his illness and had retired from practice. Gradually he became worse and spent most of his time locked in a small bedroom.

He was never really violent, but he made a lot of noise, and his shouts could be heard for some considerable distance. His wife was a delightful, silver-haired lady with twinkling blue eyes and pink cheeks. She was short and plump and blessed with a cheerful disposition.

With them lived Rose, a thin, angular, middle-aged lady whose position in the household was a cross between companion and housekeeper. In addition, she exercised the several cairn terriers and could be seen each day walking to the village carrying food and water for the other dogs which were housed in kennels rented from the Squire. All these dogs belonged to a titled lady who lived abroad and who had left them in the Gordons' care. Rose usually had two dogs on a lead, and I never remember seeing her wear anything other than a fawn raincoat with a felt hat pulled well down over her head.

Mrs Gordon was never particularly forthcoming. When asked how Mr Gordon was faring, her reply was invariably, 'Well, he's no worse!' Then she would smile, and people would marvel at her cheerfulness.

She had a married daughter who, together with husband and young daughter, would visit her from time to time. They were amiable people and if their visit coincided with a Bank Holiday, as it often did, Mrs Gordon, daughter, son-in-law and granddaughter would all attend the dance at the Village Hall, leaving Rose in charge at home. Everyone would be pleased to see Mrs Gordon out enjoying herself, and her Scots accent was a pleasant change from the flatter Midlands vernacular of the rest of us. How she enjoyed herself too, entering fully into the spirit of the evening, and how we admired the smart dresses of her daughter and granddaughter.

In the second block of council houses lived a retired

Army officer and his wife and daughter. Mother and daughter dressed smartly, and both were extremely handsome.

Christine, the daughter, was in her late teens when I first remember her. She was slim and dark-haired, her hair neatly bobbed, and she wore bright colours, always in the latest fashion. She did not go out to work, so her father must have retired on a good pension, and perhaps had some private means. At any rate, they seemed to want for nothing. Christine owned an Alsatian dog which she trained to carry a shopping basket and which no doubt one would say today 'added to her image'.

When I was about ten years old, she married a commercial traveller from Tamworth. I went along to the church to see the wedding. which was a low-key affair, on a weekday in the school holidays. Christine and her mother wore dresses of floral chiffon with large picture hats, and Christine carried a shower bouquet of carnations. After the wedding, the newlyweds lived with her parents, but no one knew much about the bridegroom, nor how Christine had come to meet him as she did not appear to go out much and certainly never participated in any of our village activities. There is nothing more aggravating than knowing a little of someone's private life and being unable to discover more. This was the case with Christine and Dick. They were personable and would chat to people but were skilful at revealing nothing. It really was most annoying for everyone.

The last house in the row was occupied by the headmistress of the village school. It stood out from the rest because the garden contained 'different' shrubs, plants and trees. In an area where everyone had daffodils and narcissi in spring, together with the odd lilac and laburnum, the end house had scyllas and anemones, lupins and buddleia and, of course, the high dividing fence was festooned with tea roses.

Every garden in the village was well cultivated and ours was no exception. Dad was always ready to try something new so he would spend many winter evenings poring over the seed catalogue before sending off for his supply. A new variety of potato guaranteed immune from this or that disease, or a pea which produced a bigger and better crop was often included on his list, in addition to the tried and trusted varieties. Naturally, vegetables and soft fruit took up a greater part of the garden, but directly in front of the house was our flower garden. Roses were Dad's great love, and he could never resist the latest variety. On many occasions, we noticed people stop to look over our front gate at the profusion of beautiful blooms. We had bush roses, standard roses of every colour, and – near the front door – Dad built rustic arches on which he trained Dorothy Perkins roses whose great clusters of fragrant blooms were a joy to behold.

Bordering the path in spring, we had blue aubretia trailing over the triangular-set bricks, and behind them were rows of red and yellow wallflowers. In summer, the wallflowers were replaced by stock and asters, with a row of red carnations at the back, and delphiniums behind the carnations.

A portion of the main garden was always reserved for sweet peas. Few gardens in the village did not boast these lovely, delicate flowers.

Sometimes, on a summer evening, a stranger would call and ask to buy a bunch of flowers. Dad would pick a huge bunch for which the passer-by would pay, perhaps, sixpence and go happily on his way.

All this, I took for granted.

The Village School

The school was the focal point of secular interest in any village and Elford was no exception. It was built by the Squire in the middle of the nineteenth century* and had changed little over the years. The lavatories were in the yard and consisted of the original earth closets. The cloakrooms had wooden pegs for coats and hats and there was an enamel basin beside which stood a large enamel jug of water. A high roller towel, which was changed once a week, hung on a wall. Boys and girls had separate entrances and separate playgrounds.

There were three classrooms - infants, middle, and older children. The infants went into the middle class at the age of six or seven, depending on how quickly they learned to read and write, whilst standards two and three went up from the middle to the big class, containing standards four to seven, at about nine or ten – again depending on ability and achievement.

School leaving age was fourteen, and, once you had achieved that birthday, there was no waiting for the end of term. We had three teachers - two of whom were qualified. The teacher of the middle class was uncertificated. There were approximately seventy children in the school, some of whom had to walk three miles to get there. There were no school dinners, so children who could not get home brought sandwiches for lunch.

---

* It was actually founded by family member, Mary Howard

In winter, the headmistress made cocoa in a huge enamel jug and each child was able to have a hot drink. It was made with considerably more water than milk but, on a wintry day, it was better than the cold water which was the midday drink in summer. Lighting, when needed, was provided by oil lamps, suspended from the ceiling, and the school was heated by huge black stoves which, while generally efficient, smoked badly on occasion.

Most boys went from the village school at fourteen to work on farms and the girls went into domestic service. Their schoolwork was geared to this end. Mornings were always devoted to book work, and we were taught in the well-tried method which stuck. Before decimalisation, I frequently used the old jingles like, 'twenty pence are one and eight, forty pence are three and four...' and so on. Similarly, I find that having been taught multiplication tables parrot fashion has stood me in good stead on many occasions. Spelling was something else on which our teachers were very keen. 'I before E, except after C, their = people, there = place'. Alright, maybe it's old-fashioned, but no child left that school unable to read, write and spell properly, or do simple arithmetic. We did a little history and geography too, and, of course, we learned how to draw and paint.

The rector came to school once a week to instruct the middle class in their catechism, and on the first Wednesday of each month, we all attended a service in church. It was unthinkable for any female to attend church in those days without wearing a hat, so we all had to remember to take one on that day. If any girl forgot... well, there was a supply of rather ancient woolly hats kept at school for just such an emergency. Be sure, few girls forgot more than once. The horror of the borrowed hat was sufficient warning.

There was no such thing as P.E., but once a week, we all filed into the Boys' playground for Drill. This consisted mainly of such exercises as, 'Heels raise, arms stretch.... and lower...', knee bending, running on the spot, and jumping, feet astride and together, and so forth.

On two afternoons a week, the middle and big classes joined forces. The girls learned to sew, knit and embroider, whilst the boys did woodwork in winter and on wet summer days, and gardening in spring and summer. On Friday afternoons, we had Community Singing, when we sang the old folk songs like, 'Cherry Ripe', 'Some Folks Do', and sea shanties such as, 'What Shall We Do With The Drunken Sailor?', 'Rio Grande', and many more.

A good part of the Christmas term was spent in preparation for the musical play that was put on for the benefit of the school and the village. These were always very gay, tuneful affairs. One year it was 'The Pied Piper', another year, 'Beauty and the Beast', One year, we presented an original called 'Princess Chrysanthemum' which was set in Japan, and we were all set to work to tie small pieces of pink crepe paper onto twigs and branches to resemble cherry blossom. The plays were performed three times. Once in an afternoon for the schoolchildren, and on two evenings for parents and friends.

The stage was built by placing planks of wood on top of desks and covering the whole with a rather elderly green carpet. The footlights were candles with the reflectors being made from cocoa tins.

I don't remember where all the 'props' were stored for the rest of the year, but I suppose it must have been in the Institute which stood near the school. This building, older than the school, had been erected by the parish for use as a meeting place and commemorated the relief of a famine in the 18th century. It was small but came in useful as a sort of overflow for the school. For instance, the boys did their woodwork there. Funny, but I don't recall who taught them to use tools, but someone must have done. Possibly the rector.

In the spring term, the school voted for a May Queen, and on each May 1st, every child arrived at school bearing a maypole. This consisted of a stick or stave often as tall as the child, on which flowers had been tied or wired. There was a competition for the best decorated one. On the night before May Day, a draw would be made in the boys' playground, and the staff and some of the older children would decorate the winning maypole with cherry blossom and whatever greenery was available. Lovely, fresh, green beech was always included. A farmer lent the dray and, on May Day itself, one of his sons, who was also a pupil, would arrive at school leading the smartly turned-out horse, brasses gleaming, and mane and tail beribboned.

A chair would be placed on the dray and, at 10 a.m., the retiring May Queen, wearing her crown of real flowers, would be seated on the chair, surrounded by her four maids. Behind her would sit the new May Queen and her four maids. All would be dressed in white, and each would have a decorated maypole. When all were properly settled, the procession would set off to tour the village. All the schoolchildren followed behind the May Queens and their attendants.

Doris in her May Queen regalia, May 1st 1932 (note the dirty knees. She had just been climbing a tree, much to her mother's dismay!)

The farmer's dray, ready to process through the village with the retiring and new May Queens (probably May 1st 1932)

The first stop was near the Hall where the Squire's lady and his sister would come out to greet us all. Then all the children would gather round to sing a May song – all traditional, old English tunes such as, 'Joan to the Maypole', 'Now is the Month of Maying' and 'Come Ye Young Men'. We trilled them all so merrily. The procession would wend its way on through the village, and, at various points, would stop for another song to be sung whilst villagers came to see and to listen.

The afternoon's activities took place on the Rectory lawn. First of all, the new May Queen, followed by her attendants, would advance to where the retiring Queen sat on her 'throne'. There she would kneel whilst the 'old' Queen removed the crown from her own head and placed it on the head of her successor. Everyone would clap as the new Queen was raised and took her place on the 'throne'.

Then, after the singing of a song for the occasion, the dancing began.

First of all, the infants danced round the maypole to the tune, 'Come Lasses and Lads' played on a rather wheezy gramophone. Then it was the turn of the older children to dance the old country dances – 'Gathering Peascods', 'Rufty Tufty, 'Sellengers Round', 'Black Nag', 'If All The World Were Paper', 'Haste to the Wedding', and others, interspersed with dancing round the maypole. Whenever I see the national dances from the Ukraine and other European countries, performed by groups in this country, I feel sad that our own country dances appear to have been largely forgotten.

We had a tall maypole which was none too firm, so four boys had to sit on the base to stop it being pulled over by the weaving in and out of the dancers.

Mayday Maypole Celebrations 1932 – Doris is the girl with long fair hair, pictured along with Billy Elson, Maud Stevenson, Reg and Phyllis Chamberlain, Eric Bott, Phyllis Purchase, Jim Ramsell, Elizabeth Harrison, Ron Rowe, Jack Clynton and Connie Usherwood

If the day happened to be wet, the procession was cancelled, and the crowning ceremony took place in the school. The two larger classrooms were made into one sizeable room by folding back the dividing doors. Of necessity, activities were rather restricted indoors, but there were, in fact, very few wet May Days as far as I remember. If May Day occurred on Saturday or Sunday, the festival was held on Monday.

The revival of the old May Festival was the brainchild of Miss Frank who was headmistress from the early 1920s. She was a traditionalist and sought to preserve and revive as many of the old ways of the countryside as practicable. She had an uncertain temper, however, and was not altogether popular. Years later we learned that she had a great liking for the national drink of Scotland, so perhaps that was partly the cause of the trouble.

There can be no doubt, however, that she cared very deeply about the children and was particularly concerned about the poorer ones. One large family of siblings had a walk of three miles morning and night and as often happens with children, occasionally forgot their sandwiches for lunch. When that happened, they were usually given some bread and jam to eat. I suspect the head paid for that herself. It sounds little enough to do, but there were six of those children in school and at least they were not allowed to go hungry. In any case, the food they brought from home also usually consisted of bread and jam.

Their mother must have been very hard-pressed, raising ten children on a farm worker's wage, even with a tied cottage and free milk and potatoes. The children's clothes came from the jumble sales held twice a year in the village school, and I remember being severely scolded by my mother after complaining to her that another girl had told Phyllis that the dress she was wearing had once been hers when I knew it was mine and told Phyllis so. I did not realize, of course, how hurtful such arguments must have been to poor Phyllis until Mother pointed it out to me. Children can be very cruel to one another.

Few people in the village had money to spare, yet they made the most of what they had, and, on the whole, children were sent to school neat and tidy. Boots and shoes were well-cleaned and, if dresses or trousers were darned or patched, they were neatly done and usually clean. Often, in the case of a younger child, a handkerchief would be secured to their front with a safety pin. Just in case.

Concerned that a number of children in the school had never seen the sea, Miss Frank organised a charabanc trip to New Brighton where a good time was had by all. It was so successful, that the following year we all went to Llandudno for the day.

When Miss Frank left, her place was taken by a teacher from Birmingham who brought more up-to-date methods with her.

She replaced the Christmas musicals with excerpts from Shakespearean plays, which few of the audience understood, but they applauded with enthusiasm. More emphasis was placed on academic subjects, but some of the old traditions were maintained.

No child had succeeded in gaining a scholarship to Tamworth High School, so she concentrated on remedying this with the result that another girl and I were given special tuition. The other girl, who was called Freda, was considered to have the best chance of a scholarship but I was with her 'for company'. To everyone's amazement, not least my own, Freda failed, and I passed. The result came on the day I was voted May Queen and I was rather dazed by the double event, but I still had to pass an oral exam so there was not too much backslapping. I had to wait a further month before I knew for certain that I would be going to the High School. Then there was great rejoicing. The Head told the school that I was the first, but she expected there would be others. What I had done, others could do, and so on… My popularity was assured when she announced an extra half-day holiday to celebrate the occasion.

There were no half-term holidays in our school, but we were given the afternoon off on Pancake Day (Shrove Tuesday). The Pancake Bell would be rung at the church at noon, and we would all hurry home to eat our pancakes with lemon and sugar.

On May 24th, we celebrated Empire Day. If the weather was fine, we would all stand in the Boys' playground and sing, 'Men of Harlech', 'Loch Lomond', 'Killarney', 'Land of Hope and Glory' and 'Three Cheers for the Red, White and Blue'. It was only many years later that I even began to wonder why we sang 'Killarney' when it was no longer part of Great Britain.

The Union Jack would flutter from the flagpole, and it was a serious, solemn occasion. If it rained, we sang our songs in the schoolroom, but we always sang with great gusto.

Elford Hall and the Last Squire

We still had a Squire living at the Hall in Elford.* He seemed ancient to me, although I don't suppose he was much over sixty. He was tall, thin and impoverished. The entire village had once belonged to his family but gradually everything that was not entailed was sold off.

The property was disposed of with great reluctance, and the Squire still kept an eye on things, going out for a walk each day to inspect what had once been his birthright.

One of the first things Dad did on moving into our house was to cut down a large yew tree in the front garden. He felt it was dangerous with children around. The Squire stood and stared at the empty gap near the hedge but, of course, beyond making his feelings plain, by glowering, there was nothing he could do. Dad later learned that no tree had previously ever been felled on the Squire's property except at his personal command.

Each winter, the Squire and his lady†, went to Torquay for three months. Usually their daughter, Charlotte, went too. She was the youngest, and only member of the family still at home. I don't remember her well, but Bill and Frank both knew her because when the rector started a Cub pack and Scout troop in the village, Miss Charlotte was the Akala.

---

* Howard Francis Paget 1858-1935
† Alice, 1863-1934

The Scoutmaster was a young farmer and, as the two got to know each other better, their friendship turned to love. The Squire was furious when he heard of it and insisted on Charlotte giving up her Scout work.

Somehow or other, the two contrived to meet, and when the Squire discovered this, Charlotte was sent to stay with her brother in South Africa. She remained there for three years, and, during all that time, she and her farmer sweetheart kept up a steady correspondence.

When she returned and found her father still refusing permission for her to marry, she and the young man eloped. They went to the West Country and were married by special licence by a clergyman friend of the family who, though very willing to perform the ceremony, insisted on Charlotte telephoning her father and telling him of her intentions in order to give him time to give his blessing.

The old Squire acknowledged his defeat, saying sadly, 'It wasn't money I wanted for my daughter. It was a name.'

Of course, the news went round the village like wildfire, and everyone was enchanted with the romance. Much better than anything in *Home Notes* or *Peg's Paper*.

Despite the Squire's misgivings, the marriage turned out well and Charlotte found no difficulty becoming an efficient farmer's wife.

The Squire's lady was a delightful person. I recall her dressed mostly in grey and violet colours with lots of velvet and chiffon.

Frank was often involved in mischievous goings-on in the village, and she called him 'the scamp'. She was fond of him because she said he could put on a look of such wide-eyed innocence that, until one got to know him, no one would imagine him capable of any misdemeanour. Mind you, as people got to know him even better, he was frequently suspected of pranks in which he had no hand.

There were several boys all about the same age at the village school. They must have been a great trial to the headmistress and one day she ordered three of them, including Frank, to stay behind after school to plant out some wallflowers in the school garden. I don't recall what the punishment was for, but they evidently felt a sense of injustice because they carefully planted all the wallflowers upside down, with the roots sticking up in the air. When she saw what they had done, her face turned purple with fury, but she decided to get the rector to deal with them. As it was a church school, he was partly responsible for its smooth running.

It was through the rector that Mother got to learn of the upside-down wallflowers. He called on her after he had talked to the delinquents, and Mother said she thought he would never stop laughing. Of course, he had tried to show the boys the error of their ways, but it had not been easy for him, with his acute sense of the ridiculous. Needless to say, Mother did not tell Frank the rector was amused.

Once a year there was a sale of work at the Hall in aid of the Society for the Propagation of the Gospel (S.P.G.). Everyone in the village was expected to support it and usually did so. In school, the girls had sewn, embroidered and knitted all year towards this event and the boys had been busy with woodwork. In addition, there were cakes from the Mothers' Union, sweets, books and the inevitable bran tub.

Frank had threepence and I had one penny pocket money each week and we used to save some of it to spend at the sale. On this particular day, Mother had bought the iron holder that I had made, and the serviette ring and stool made by Frank, plus a framed photograph of the Hall and a jar of local honey.

The following day, the Squire's lady called on Mother and gave her a book called *Sambo's Saturday Night**. It was a thin paperback and she had been standing near the bookstall the previous afternoon when Frank had come up to look. He had picked up that particular book and enquired the price.

'Sixpence,' said the lady in charge.

'Oh,' said Frank, 'I've only got fourpence left,' and he went away, looking dejected.

The Squire's lady said the look of disappointment on his face had touched her so deeply that she had promptly bought the book herself and was now bringing it for him.

It was spontaneous acts of kindness like that which endeared her to everyone in the village. She delighted in knowing all the children by name and encouraged them to visit her. Despite her elevated position in the village, she was far more approachable than some of the farmers' wives who had inflated ideas of their own importance as land-owning families and employers of labour. Furthermore, she was a much kinder employer. Her servants left only to get married, and those who grew old in her service were given rooms at the Hall in which to end their days. She really cared about people and was greatly loved in return.

---

* Please remember, this was long before attitudes – and language – became more enlightened

The Squire and his lady died within a few months of each other, and the heir had little interest in the village. He had quarrelled with his father many years previously, walked out and had never returned to the Hall afterwards. Rumour had it that he had been cut off without the proverbial shilling, but of course the old Squire could do nothing to prevent the entail passing to the eldest son.

The new Squire had no intention of living in Elford and he could not sell the property, so he gave it away to the first big city prepared to accept it.

The village regretted it but there was no way of stopping it and thus another era ended. Forty years on, the Hall had fallen into decay and was demolished.†

---

† Please note, the fate of Elford Hall is told here from Doris's perception, which seems to have been shared by many in the village at the time. The Paget family account differs somewhat in the detail. The fundamental facts remain the same. The son and heir – Francis Howard Paget – did gift the Hall to the City of Birmingham who were poor custodians, allowing the Hall to fall into a state of dereliction, resulting in its demolition. The gardens, however, have been rescued and restored by a group of hardworking, dedicated volunteers – The Elford Hall Garden Project elfordhallgarden.org

The Village Hall

Dad took an active interest in everything connected with the village and was soon on the Parish Council.

At this time, there was only one place in the village where meetings and social functions could be held – the school. Clearly, a Village Hall was badly needed, and a committee was formed under the chairmanship of the rector. This soon struck problems however, because the rector wanted the Hall to be built on church-owned ground so that the church would have the major say in anything to do with the Hall. Many people could foresee problems with such an arrangement. For starters, it would mean that there could be no social functions during Lent. The proposal was rejected, and the rector promptly resigned (from the committee) along with the churchwarden and sexton. Eventually, a new committee was formed under the chairmanship of Mr Porter, a Birmingham businessman who lived in a beautiful house near the centre of the village. Dad was a member of the committee and meetings were held at Mr Porter's house.

We got to know Mr and Mrs Porter very well. He came often to our house. I used to be invited to have tea with Mrs Porter on my way home from school. She had a large grey parrot called Polly and a cairn terrier called Andy. The two were sworn enemies. Tea with Mrs Porter was usually an eventful occasion, and I don't ever remember having much to eat. Most of the time seemed to be taken up with separating the two belligerents.

On one dreadful occasion, Polly managed to land on Andy's back and clung on, swearing furiously as the poor dog charged frantically round the drawing room, banging into furniture in an endeavour to dislodge the unwelcome jockey. When Mrs Porter managed to pluck Polly from her 'perch', there were two red, bald patches on Andy's back and great tufts of dog hair in the parrot's claws. Polly was chained to her proper perch after that little episode.

The first Village Hall c.1931

The Village Hall committee organised various fundraising activities in the schoolroom and bought some land in the centre of the village. At the end of two long years, they had raised sufficient capital to build the Hall and erected a wooden building with diamond pane windows, which fitted in well with its surroundings.

The grand opening was a truly memorable occasion. Music came from the Hollywood Dance Band who travelled over from nearby Alrewas. All the ladies who attended wore new dresses, and the men donned their best navy blue. Admission was one and sixpence.

It was decided that a weekly dance would be held, admission sixpence, every Friday night. For this, Mrs Wallis, the railway signalman's wife, played the piano, alternating with Mr Green, the railway linesman, on the melodeon. These dances proved popular and were well attended.

On Boxing Day, Easter Monday and Whit Monday, as well as various times in between, there would be a Grand Dance when the men wore their best suits and the ladies their prettiest dresses. Summer Dances, like the one on August Bank Holiday Monday, were billed as Flannel Dances and men wore sports jackets and flannels, but the girls usually wore their best dresses to those as well. Admission, where a proper band was playing, never cost more than one and sixpence. There were always plenty of refreshments, with tea at one penny a cup and large ham sandwiches at threepence each. Fizzy lemonade at a penny a big glass and fancy cakes were also available, but no intoxicating liquor of any kind. If you wanted that, you nipped out to *The Crown*, but not many people bothered.

The men of the Committee took turns at being on the door, and admission was always strictly by ticket only. If anyone wanted to pop out during the dance, he or she was given one half of a ticket to enable them to re-enter. It did not matter how well one was known to the person selling the tickets, the rules were firmly adhered to. There was never any trouble of any kind.

The doors were firmly closed at ten p.m. so that anyone who had spent the evening at the pub was not allowed in, even with a ticket. An exception was made for Mr and Mrs Rowe, the landlord and his wife, since it was their job which had kept them away until 'closing time'.

Whist Drives and dances were popular and always attracted many people young and old. And there was a variety of other entertainments. Mr and Mrs Porter's house-parlourmaid, tired of going into Tamworth every Saturday night, got together a group of nine and ten-year-olds. We rehearsed little playlets and poems and put on a concert at the end of the summer. Then there were visiting concert parties, of a uniformly high standard. All amateur of course, and all good clean fun with plenty of audience participation.

Every August Bank Holiday morning, it was time for the annual village flower show. Dad always took the prize with his roses, but no one could touch the Servin brothers with their vegetables. They exhibited their produce at all the village shows for miles around and must have won a lot of money each year. They were great gardeners and never exhibited anything they had not grown themselves but, as happens in every small community, their continuing success caused a certain amount of jealous comment from those who went away empty. Some suggested that perhaps it would be a good idea for the gardens of competitors to be inspected before the show. The brothers readily agreed, and nothing further was done about it.

There was always a mad scramble at five o'clock to get the Hall cleared of flowers and vegetables ready for the evening dance, due to start at eight o'clock. Dad used to come home, puffing and panting, to wash, shave and change, and off we would go again, to dance until two in the morning. Yes, the children went as well if their parents liked to take them. I cannot remember a time when I could not waltz or foxtrot or do the veleta or military two-step. I suppose we must have been a bit of a nuisance to the adults, but I don't think anyone complained. Everyone was too intent on enjoying the evening, and country folk were a tolerant lot on the whole.

St Peter's Church

The village church in Elford played an important part in the life of the community. It was a beautiful little church with a square tower. Dedicated to St Peter, it had the Squire as its patron, and his family had their own special part of the church, rather than a separate chapel, with tombs and memorials to their ancestors.

The pulpit was made of wood and beautifully carved, and the font had a magnificently carved dark oak cover, almost like a steeple.

It was always warm in winter; the heating supplied by a boiler in the basement – I don't think anyone called it a crypt. The warmth came up through ornamental gratings in the aisles. Enormous chandeliers provided the lighting, although these were not the usual glittering crystal affairs one usually associates with that word. They were, in fact, rather like tiered iron cartwheels, containing cups for hundreds of candles. Unfortunately, if you were directly beneath one of them, you might come away with candle grease on your shoulders but, otherwise, the lighting was soft and quite adequate. Strangers to the village found this form of illumination fascinating as most village churches were lit by oil lamps in those days. A mourner at a funeral was heard to remark after the service that he hadn't heard a word the rector had said as he had spent his time endeavouring to count the candles.

The rector* was a man in his mid-thirties and, like many country parsons of the time, had a private income, so the upkeep of the huge rectory and garden presented him with no real problems. He had been a padre in the Great War, was wounded, and married the young V.A.D. who had nursed him. Elford was his first post-war living. They had two small children and employed a governess to teach them.

Mrs Prince, who was the sister of the rector's wife, lived at the rectory. She was an elegant and gracious lady and took over a good deal of parish visiting. Her husband, a brilliant veterinary surgeon, was in a mental home. He had been showing violent tendencies for a long time, but she had coped reasonably well, until one evening when he attempted to shoot her with his old army service revolver. Fortunately, his aim had been wild, and he had been overpowered by the butler and another manservant. This time, doctors insisted that, for his own and everyone else's safety, Mr Prince must be put in a mental institution.

Mrs Prince was extremely popular in the village and made herself as much at home in the tiny, bare kitchen of the poorest cottager as in the most prosperous farmer's sitting room. If she knew of a household where a mother or a child was sick, she would often take a little delicacy to tempt a poor appetite, but there was none of the patronage so often attached to such acts of kindness in those days. She came as a friend and was accepted as such. No woman caught in the middle of a dirty job felt any embarrassment about inviting her into their home. In fact, she had been known to

---

* Rev Bridson

lend a hand on more than one occasion. Mrs Prince had the knack of being able to do such things without losing any of the respect villagers felt for the rector and his family.

The rector was popular with everyone as he had a modern outlook towards religion, believing it should be a joyful way of living, and that to be a good Christian one did not have to be miserable. He was particularly interested in the younger people. He marked out a tennis court on the rectory lawn and taught them to play tennis, lending them racquets and balls from his own collection. He taught the boys to play cricket too.

The rectory was bordered on one side by the river, so the rector had a punt, and we youngsters enjoyed many a happy ride on fine summer afternoons during school holidays.

During winter evenings, the rector formed a group called the King's Messengers. I am not sure if such an organisation exists today, and I am certainly not at all clear on the exact purpose of it‡. We used to meet one evening a week in the winter months, from six until seven o'clock. These meetings were held in a room in the servants' quarters of the (Elford) Hall, and we were usually under the care of the rectory governess, although, once in a while, the rector himself took us in hand. We used to hear stories of the 'heathens' in darkest Africa and how the missionaries were helping them to become aware of the word of God, so that they didn't eat each other anymore!

There was great excitement one evening because the rector had received a letter from one of these missionaries

---

† The King's Messengers was the children's branch of the aforementioned S.P.G. and had been formed in 1891. Following a name change to Adventurers, it was eventually disbanded, probably during the 1960s.

that concerned him deeply. We had made a patchwork quilt and sent it to this man, who had been delighted with it. He was even more grateful a few months later, when the settlement in which he lived was raided by fierce-looking 'savage tribesmen', who grabbed him and demanded gifts. The only thing he could offer of any worth was his patchwork quilt. He handed it over, and the leader of the raiding party was so delighted that he draped it round his shoulders and wore it as a cloak. The missionary assured us that our patchwork quilt had saved his life!

There was one point with which a few parishioners – Mother amongst them – disagreed with the rector. He was inclined towards Anglo-Catholicism and introduced incense. One of the stalwarts of his choir was William Williams, a carpenter in the village. Mother said, very crossly, after the choir had processed round the church during the Harvest Festival service, that she was sure he gave the censer an extra swing when he got near her, just because he knew she didn't like it. Indeed, there were so many protests that this 'High Church' practice had to be abandoned. It was emptying the pews rapidly.

Believing sincerely that 'confession is good for the soul', the rector also attempted to introduce the confessional. There was, however, an even greater storm of protest over this, so he decided to confine it to people who were being prepared for confirmation. My brother, Frank, was one of them, and Mother forbade him to go to confession. A few young people did go, but reduced it to such a farce that this too was discontinued.

I have happy memories of both Sunday School as an infant and catechism in church as an older child. The rector himself was in charge of the latter, and we always began with the hymn, 'Our Blessed Redeemer' which, even today, remains my favourite hymn*. Every Sunday School pupil had a card and each week we were given a stamp to stick on it. The picture on the stamp was relevant to the particular period in the church calendar. If, through illness or holiday, a child was unable to attend, they would receive an 'Unavoidably Absent' stamp. I was often fortunate in that I used to go with my cousin, Kathleen, to her Sunday School when we were staying with her family in Tibberton, and sometimes they had the same issue of stamps, so I was able to dispense with the uninteresting 'Unavoidably Absent'. The boys and girls with the greatest number of stamps on their cards received a prize at the end of each year.

A good number of children also attended Matins at eleven o'clock and we had our own special pews, as did the grown-ups.

The maids from Elford Hall sat on the south aisle, with two elderly retired retainers immediately behind them.

The rector's wife and children, together with their governess and the rector's sister-in-law occupied a pew at the front near the pulpit.

But the most jealously guarded pews were those the children occupied. Most of us sat on the north aisle. Those were days when children were seen and not heard. Little ones learned from a very early age to be quiet in church. They learned the hard way. A cuff from an older child is far more effective than any rebuke from a parent. Our

---

* This was sung at Doris's funeral in 2018, as she requested.

favourite occupation during the sermon was to construct a rabbit from our handkerchiefs. I tried to do that recently, but it was hopeless, and, after a dozen attempts, I gave up, yet I doubt if any churchgoing child in Elford found any difficulty—at any rate in my day.

It was soon after the disagreement over the Village Hall that the rector left Elford. No one wanted him to go but he felt, rightly or wrongly, that he had lost the trust of his parishioners, and moved to the south of England. The new rector was a very different type. He came from the Coventry diocese and had no private income. His wife dressed far more shabbily than anyone else in the village and the rector himself looked ill-cared for and untidy. They found the heating at the rectory quite beyond their means, so shivered throughout the winter in the large rooms.

From being a comfortable family home, the rectory degenerated into a neglected, forlorn house. Only the former servants' quarters were occupied because the rector's wife said that, as the cooking stove was there, they might as well live there and save fuel. They never used the central heating boiler, and they employed no domestic outdoor help. The garden quickly became a wilderness, and the rector fought a losing battle with the once-velvety lawns.

The churchyard suffered too. This had always been mown regularly by the former rector, but poor Mr Tuff, the new incumbent, was a much older man and just could not cope.

As in most villages, the parish sat back and took its time to decide if it approved of their new rector. They decided he, 'wasn't a patch on the last one', and only the most dedicated continued to go regularly to church. Mr Tuff possessed a monotonous voice and his sermons lacked interest. He was, in fact, quite out of tune with rural life, having always lived in an industrial city.

He spent a lot of time telling everyone in Elford who would listen, how fortunate they were to live in such surroundings and that the people of his last parish were far poorer. As most of our people were themselves living simply, they did not take kindly to such remarks. In any case, most of them having lived in Elford all their lives, as had their parents and grandparents before them, felt they had little need of advice from a stranger on how to appreciate their own village.

What really set the cat among the pigeons though was when Mrs Tuff, discovering that the Mothers' Union Fund had a healthy credit balance, decided to use some of the money to buy material which she cut up into garments and handed out to members to sew. This was not unusual. The mothers had done this sort of thing in the past and the garments had then been sold at the annual sale of the S.P.G., so it came as a shock, therefore, when they learned that, this time, the finished garments would be sent to the parish the Tuffs had just left.

There was resentment among the members, many of whom could themselves have made good use of some of the things. Eventually, Mrs Senlow, a railwayman's wife and never one to pull her punches, voiced the feelings of them all in no uncertain manner. She said it was time Mrs Tuff concentrated on the needy of Elford and left the people of her last parish to their present vicar's wife. In fact, if she, Mrs Senlow, was that lady she would not take too kindly to interference from Mrs Tuff.

When Mrs Tuff had recovered from her shock, she was, to say the least, very 'put out' and said so. Several of the mothers then collected their belongings and marched out. After a little while, the embarrassed remainder sheepishly followed, leaving Mrs Tuff to wonder what on earth she had done.

Much to her chagrin, Mother missed that particular meeting, being in bed with pleurisy at the time. She received a full report from my godmother who had been there.

There were doubts that the Mothers' Union could survive such a fracas. However, the following month, more members than usual turned up, but there no sewing was handed out and nothing more was heard of the 'poor of the last parish'.

It transpired that someone had dropped a word in the ear of the Squire's lady and she, tactful woman that she was, had 'had a talk' with Mrs Tuff.

No one could really understand how it was that the Rev. Tuff had been appointed to the living of Elford. After all, the Squire, as patron, had a great say in who should be rector. Perhaps the old man felt sorry for Mr Tuff. Whatever the reason, the Tuffs stayed for ten or more years, and the village learned to live with them, though they never really took to them as they had to their predecessors.

When the couple did eventually leave, it was to go into retirement in a house in the Cathedral Close, Lichfield.

EDITOR'S NOTE

This is the end of my mother's main account of her childhood in Elford. The family moved to Tamworth in 1934 following a year living in a Birmingham suburb where her mother and brother, Frank, ran a small shop. I believe the move from Elford may have been precipitated by my grandfather's health. It was around this time that Jack Buttery became seriously ill from perforated gastric ulcers and required a major operation to remove a significant portion of his stomach. Naturally, he was incapacitated for some considerable time, and they were living in a tied cottage so would not have been able to stay there. Perhaps understandably, my mother chose never to write about these difficult times and, indeed, rarely mentioned them when I was growing up.

PART TWO
A Tale of Two Brothers

Introduction

Some years after Mum ceased her general village memoirs, she once again picked up her trusty pen, pencil and foolscap pad, and turned her attention to writing specifically about her two older brothers – William (known initially as Billy and then, for most of his life, Bill) who was born in 1909, and George Frank (always known as Frank), born in 1913.

She was nearest to Frank in age – albeit she was seven years younger – and closest in terms of temperament and personality in general. Bill, on the other hand, at eleven years her senior, had little in common with his little sister although, towards the end of his life, he and Mum became quite close. But there is no doubting Mum was closest to Frank, even though, in the late 1940s, he elected to take his wife and six-year-old son, John, to Bulawayo, in what was then known as Southern Rhodesia (now Zimbabwe). He had obtained a position at the Rhodesian Iron and Steel Corporation, where he worked for a number of years, and was never to return to the U.K. As a result, Mum did not see her brother again although they kept in touch via fairly regular airmail correspondence, and Mum became a much-loved godmother to Susan, my cousin, whom she finally met in 1972 when Sue made a trip to England.

Here then, are Mum's recollections of growing up with two older brothers. From certain references she makes, and paper she uses, I estimate she wrote this account down, in stages, during the 1970s.

Ann Nibbs, Editor

Bill

I hadn't thought of Lily Hobbs for years, yet it came as something of a shock to read her name in the Obituary column of the *Tamworth Herald*. Although I have not lived in Tamworth for well over twenty years, I still have many friends there whom I visit from time to time, and I have the *Herald* sent by post each week. Inevitably when you are an 'exile'*, it is to the Births, Marriages and Deaths one first turns and so it was on this occasion as I settled down with my elevenses.

Lily Hobbs, I thought. Of course, her name hadn't been Hobbs for fifty years, not since she married a man called Brotherton and moved to Coventry for a time, but she'll always be Lily Hobbs to me. She was beautiful and to my adoring eight-year-old eyes, she was elegant. I put down the paper and gazed dreamily into the past.

In Elford, it was more or less taken for granted that, on completing school at fourteen, most boys would work on a farm and most girls would go into domestic service.

My oldest brother, Bill, wasn't having that. He, who used to wear gloves to weed the garden, got himself taken on as an apprentice at a garage in Tamworth and, as Dad afterwards remarked, was 'never so happy as when he was up to his ears in muck.' Frank, by contrast, was the brainy member of the family. He won a scholarship to a business

---

* Doris had moved away from Tamworth upon her marriage in 1949.

college in Birmingham when he was thirteen and ended up as an accountant.

At the time Bill was nearing the end of his apprenticeship, there was great excitement in our house because he was bringing his young lady to tea. It was the first time I had ever laid eyes on Lily Hobbs.

I was her slave from the moment she smiled at me when Bill brought her in. I couldn't take my eyes off her. She wore a ruby red coat, with fur collar and cuffs and a matching hat on her black, curly hair. When she took off her coat and I saw the red dress underneath, I was enchanted. It was low-waisted in accordance with the fashion of the time, and short, but not as short as the mini-skirts that became so popular in the 1960s and thereafter. As she raised her hands to remove her hat, her skirt rose slightly and I caught a brief glimpse of a rose-coloured fancy, satin garter. Lily wore a long string of ivory-coloured beads with a matching bangle. Her earrings were red, probably garnets, that swung and glittered when she moved her head.

Lily was a sort of companion-cum-lady's maid to Mrs Bourne, a wealthy widow in Tamworth. She was paid a fairly good wage and, in addition, had plenty of free time. She dressed smartly, and I once heard Mother remark that Lily certainly knew what suited her in the way of clothes. She was as tall as Bill, slender and elegant.

Bill took her to all the local dances, and, in those days, there was a dance somewhere in the locality at least three nights in the week. Her employer was quite agreeable to her being out late on two nights a week and she was allowed to sleep at home every Saturday night as Sunday was her day off. All things considered, Lily had an enviably agreeable job.

In addition to Lily, Mrs Bourne employed a cook, a kitchen-maid and a house-parlourmaid and, of course, a full-time gardener. Mother used often to say that she never knew what they all found to occupy them, and that she hoped they all realized how well off they were. I think they must have done because Lily had never worked anywhere else, and the others had been with Mrs Bourne for many years. Indeed, they stayed with her until they were redirected into work of 'national importance' during the Second World War. All except Lily, of course. She was married before then.

Lily's father was head gardener at a big estate in Wigginton and they lived in a pleasant house for which they paid no rent. There were three girls in the family. All had flowery names. Lily was the oldest, then came Marigold – two years younger – and the youngest, Rose, a bubbly sixteen-year-old. People often remarked that Lily and Marigold should have changed names because Marigold was as fair as her sister was dark. She was not as strikingly beautiful as Lily, but had a sort of magnetism, and the first time I met her, I was aware of it.

Sometimes Frank would go along with Bill and Lily and, with Marigold making up the four, and off they would go to a dance together. Quite often there would be a Whist Drive before the dance and both my brothers seemed to be lucky in winning prizes which they often as not presented to Mother. She did well for brass candlesticks, plant bowls—she called them jardinieres—and fruit spoons. By this time, Bill had acquired a small car. It apparently had a sound engine, but in general appearance, it looked every day of its advanced age.

By the time Bill was twenty-one, in 1930, we all accepted Lily as a member of the family and took it for granted that one day she and Bill would marry. Bill had finished his apprenticeship but seemed in no hurry to put an engagement ring on Lily's finger. In those days young people were often engaged for two years or sometimes much longer, but Bill seemed content to carry on, unengaged, indefinitely.

Lily began to get restless. She was a year older than my brother, and I heard her hinting to Mother that perhaps she and Bill ought to start looking for a house. Apparently, it wasn't the first time she had voiced that thought, for I overheard Mother and Dad talking one September evening. They were fond of Lily and Mother was afraid that if Lily tried to push too hard, she would scare Bill away. Dad was agreeing with her when Frank burst in to announce that he had just seen Marigold in Bill's car. Mother shrugged this off by saying she expected Bill had merely been giving Marigold a lift somewhere, but Frank said he couldn't think where, because they were parked in Green Lane. I crept silently into the room in time to see the look of consternation which passed between my parents. Frank noticed it too.

'There,' he exclaimed, triumphantly, 'That's different, isn't it?'

Green Lane was the village Lovers' Lane and did not really lead anywhere.

Dad thoughtfully filled his pipe, while Mother clucked and said, 'I don't know I'm sure,' several times.

Frank looked from one to the other, and then sat down, apparently deflated because his news had failed to produce the anticipated volcanic reaction. I hardly dared to breathe in case somebody suddenly remembered I was there and packed me off on some unnecessary errand.

When his pipe was going to his satisfaction, Dad said calmly, 'There could be any number of reasons for it.' He puffed thoughtfully. 'It will soon be Lily's birthday so maybe they were talking about some sort of surprise for her.'

'Well, anyway,' Frank snorted. 'It looked funny to me, and at the dance in Alrewas last week, Bill danced with Marigold as often as he danced with Lily. Their mother was helping with the refreshments, and I heard her telling the other ladies it was only because Marigold didn't have a young man of her own. But it didn't look like that to me. It looked as if Bill was really enjoying himself dancing with her.'

Dad said, 'I should think any young fellow would enjoy dancing with Marigold.'

'Of course they would,' Mother put in quickly, 'I'm sure Mrs Hobbs was right, and I think it was very nice of Bill as you had got Nancy with you and couldn't oblige.'

Frank had recently taken a fancy to Nancy Rowe, daughter of the landlord of our village pub. But my brother wasn't going to let this go. 'Then why was Mrs Hobbs telling Marigold off afterwards for dancing so much with Bill?'

'How do you know that?' demanded Mother crossly.

'I heard her. I was out at the back waiting for Bill. He said he'd give me a lift home as Nancy's father hadn't room in his car. Mrs Hobbs and Marigold were in the kitchen, and the window was open. She said Marigold ought to leave Bill alone because he was Lily's property, and Marigold said it wasn't her fault if Bill liked her better than Lily.'

'You'd no business listening,' said Mother, in a reproachful tone. 'Where were Bill and Lily?'

Frank grinned. 'Saying goodnight in the front room.'

'Well, there you are then,' said Mother smugly. 'If Lily didn't mind Bill dancing with Marigold, I don't see why anyone else should.'

Frank shrugged. 'Don't know about that. Lily didn't seem too happy when Bill shared Marigold's umbrella back to the house. He had Marigold on one arm and Lily on the other. Bill and Marigold were laughing, but Lily wasn't.'

Mother turned and caught sight of me. 'Bedtime,' she said, in a voice that warned me I'd better not argue.

I was miserable. I liked Marigold, but I loved Lily and the thought of anything coming between her and Bill was more than I could bear. Mother, however, refused to discuss it when she came to kiss me goodnight, beyond warning me not to say anything to Bill - or anyone else for that matter.

Lily still came to tea at least once a week and went with Bill to all the winter dances, but I couldn't help noticing that, instead of Frank begging a lift, Bill actually asked him to go along with them in the car.

Then one day, Bill dropped a bombshell. 'I've got a job in Birmingham and I'm moving into digs there,' he announced one Saturday morning.

Mother, who was just serving up rabbit pie, paused with spoon in hand. Frank and I stared at Bill whilst Dad said quietly, 'That's a bit sudden, isn't it? When are you going and where?'

Bill took a deep breath. 'I saw an advertisement in the *Birmingham Mail* for a newly qualified man, so I applied, and they offered me the job. It's good money and I'll get more experience.'

Mother carried on serving us all with our pie, and I handed round the vegetables. We all ate in silence for a few minutes, then she said, 'What does Lily think about it?'

Bill flushed and said, 'I haven't told her yet.'

Dad looked up quickly but said nothing.

Mother gasped. 'Well, don't you think you should?'

Bill looked uncomfortable and continued to eat. After a moment, he muttered, 'I'll tell her tonight.'

❋ ❋ ❋

When Bill moved out, we heard regularly from him, and Lily came often to see us. Mother and Dad always made her very welcome, and Frank usually saw her safely home if she came in the evening. One weekend morning, when Bill was home, he and Frank stayed talking in the bedroom they shared. We were half-way through breakfast before they put in an appearance.

'What time are you going to fetch Lily?' Mother asked.

'I'm not,' replied Bill, helping himself to marmalade.

Dad flashed Mother a warning look and she bit back whatever she was about to say. A little while later, I heard him asking Bill if Lily knew he was home that weekend, and Bill said he didn't know. Dad said no more.

Bill and Frank went out somewhere that Saturday night and returned after I had gone to bed. After Bill had gone back to Birmingham, Mother tackled Frank, but he refused to divulge whatever it was he and his brother had discussed. He insisted it was of no importance. Mother knew better but was quite unable to drag anything out of Frank.

'I don't know,' she said to Dad later. 'What am I going to say to Lily next time she calls?'

'Say nothing,' advised Dad. 'It's none of our business and they're old enough to know their own minds.'

'That's the trouble,' Mother said. 'Lily does, and she wants to marry Bill. I know she does.'

'Well, if Bill doesn't want to marry Lily, there's nothing we, nor anyone else, can or should do about it,' replied Dad in a tone that inferred the subject was closed.

Mother looked at him with a troubled face. Dad patted her hand. 'Bill is too young to settle down yet. He wants to get somewhere first. It's my opinion Lily tried to rush things, and no man will stand for that.'

Mother sighed. 'I think you're probably right.'

Over the next few weeks, we saw Lily occasionally, but it was noticeable that she took to waylaying Dad on his way home from work so that he felt bound to invite her in, and they arrived at the house together. Nothing was ever said about Bill having been home, and, as she usually called during the week, it was unlikely she would turn up on a Saturday or Sunday if Bill happened to be there unexpectedly. Mother relaxed and when, after a time, Lily stopped telling us when she'd heard from Bill, no one made any comment.

We hadn't seen Lily for three weeks when Bill turned up unexpectedly one Saturday. We were all delighted to see him of course and he was chasing me round, trying to grab my pigtails when suddenly we were aware that the others had stopped laughing. Lily stood in the doorway. Bill flushed dark-red and straightened his tie. No one spoke for what seemed ages.

Then Dad said, briskly, 'Well come on in Lily, you're just in time for tea.'

She hesitated only briefly, then moved towards Bill and, putting her hands on his shoulders, kissed him full on the mouth.

I stared, fascinated, as anger spread across my brother's face. I'd never seen him look like that before. He strode out of the room, got into his car and was gone before any of us realized his intention.

Lily's face crumpled. Mother put an arm around her and helped her to a chair. I went to her and put my arms round her. I didn't know what it was all about, but I did know my goddess was terribly hurt. Lily blew her nose and gently released herself from my grapevine-like grip. Frank shifted from one foot to the other, not looking at Lily. Then he too disappeared. Mother sent me off to take some eggs to my godmother and, when I got back, Lily had gone.

When Frank came in, Mother said she supposed Bill had gone back to Birmingham, but Frank said he hadn't and that he would be back later. He was, and, amazingly, he brought Lily with him. She seemed subdued, although Bill was quiet and did not look angry anymore.

Mother prepared some supper and, afterwards, I was sent off to bed as usual. I didn't sleep though, and after a time, I heard the gramophone. No one had bought any new records for some time, so I was familiar with the ones I heard. Then I heard footsteps up and down the stairs and soon a song I'd never heard before came wafting upstairs. I was just thinking it was a nice, catchy tune when the vocal refrain started.

'I've finished with Lily forever.
I've finished for good and all...'

I caught my breath. How could Bill be so cruel? I crept to the top of the stairs as the record ended.

Bill was speaking. 'It's one of the catchiest tunes I've heard for a long time. When did you buy it, Frank?'

So that was it! Frank, always ripe for mischief, had bought it. I wondered if Mother and Dad had known about it. There was no malice in Frank, so I couldn't think that he had really meant to hurt Lily's feelings, and yet...

To my amazement, I heard Bill say, 'Put it on again, Frank,' and once again I listened, fascinated, as the record was played a second time.

There was a small silence when it ended. Someone closed the lid of the gramophone.

Then Lily said she had better be getting back as she'd told her mother she wouldn't be late. Again, there was silence and how I wished I could see instead of just hear what was going on.

After what seemed ages, I heard chairs being pushed back and then Bill said, 'Coming for the ride, Frank?' and my brother said he thought he might as well.

There seemed to be little else to hear and I knew from experience that I was in imminent danger of being caught on the stairs, so I scurried back to bed.

Next afternoon, I searched through the records until I found the one I wanted. I wound up the gramophone and listened again as a man's voice carolled the words,

'I've finished with Lily forever...'

Mother came in, looking flustered. 'I don't like that song very much,' she said, 'and if I was Lily, I'd have put on *Mean to Me* straight away after Bill had played it.'

'Why?'

'Well…because…' Mother's voice tailed off.

'Because, what?' I persisted.

'Oh,' Mother said. 'Just because!'

I could see I was going to get nothing else out of her, so I went in search of Frank, but he and Bill had disappeared in Bill's car.

We didn't see Lily again for some time, but one day, Marigold and Rose cycled over to see Mother and told her that Lily was in hospital and had 'burst a blood vessel'.

Mother was most concerned and asked a lot of questions, but, apparently, the girls could tell her little else. A week or two later, however, Mrs Hobbs called to see Mother, and I was bundled unceremoniously out of the room. As Frank was around, I didn't dare try to eavesdrop.

It was ten or fifteen years later that I learned that Lily had suffered a miscarriage and when Dad tackled Bill about it, he admitted that he was responsible for her pregnancy, but that she had 'driven him mad'. It was because of that incident – and Bill insisted it had only happened once – that he decided to break away from her. She had told him of her condition and said he would 'have to marry her', but he wasn't ready to marry anyone yet, although he promised to help in any other way.

Lily had gambled everything and lost.

We did not see Lily again for several years, but the announcement of her marriage three years later appeared in the *Tamworth Herald*, followed about a year later by the news of the birth of her daughter.

One day, Mother and I met her as we were shopping in Tamworth. She looked just the same and her baby had her dark curls and beautiful eyes.

Bill meanwhile drifted light-heartedly through several romances, finally marrying a girl some years younger than himself. They returned to live in Elford as Bill pulled off an excellent job with his old firm.

His wife's name was Peggy, and she was what we used to call, a 'peroxided blonde'. We felt Bill could have chosen better but made her welcome. From the start she showed who was going to rule the roost. She had not been used to much money of her own and the fact that Bill was doing quite well went to her head. She bought clothes quite unsuitable for country living, sent all washing to the laundry, and settled down to a life of leisure. It was a severe shock when she found out she was going to have a baby, but to give her due credit, she soon got used to the idea and launched herself into a baby trousseau-buying spree. For herself, she bought beautiful maternity smocks.

In those (pre-NHS) days, most young women gave birth at home, with the district midwife and, possibly, a doctor in attendance, while mother and mother-in-law did the chores. That was not for Peggy. She booked into the more expensive of Tamworth's two private Nursing Homes and had her baby in style, afterwards sitting up in her bed, with a filmy bedjacket round her shoulders and her face perfectly made-up while she graciously received her visitors.

At the time I thought it romantic and that it was lovely that Bill could afford all this luxury for his wife. I found out later that he couldn't. He was certainly earning what Mother called 'good money', but not quite that good.

When the baby was a year old, they moved to the South of England where a second son was born. Mother and Dad went to visit them and came back to report that things were rather different now. Peggy did her own laundry and, although she still dressed fashionably, she was not able to afford the expensive clothes she had previously bought.

Mother suspected, even so, that more was spent on clothes for herself than on things like bed linen, but Peggy seemed genuinely fond of the children and dressed them well. They looked healthy and happy, which was more than could always be said for Bill.

In fact, my parents were troubled to see him looking exhausted and run down. Mother was particularly upset to find he possessed only one suit. He worked a lot of overtime, which accounted for his tiredness, but although on the surface, Peggy and Bill seemed happy, and certainly Bill fussed over his wife to an almost sickening degree, Mother and Dad felt that this was possibly as much to reassure himself as anything else.

Peggy never really changed, and when the boys were of school age, she started going out in the evenings, leaving Bill to cope at home. The Second World War was over, not that it had affected them too much as Bill was in a reserved occupation and Peggy made it perfectly clear that she was not having him volunteer for the armed services despite his great longing to do so. Both Frank and I were in uniform from the outbreak, and Bill felt very much the 'odd man out', but he was still the besotted husband.

They were so far away from us that we saw them infrequently, but, when we did, they seemed quite happy and, although both Frank and I felt that Bill was far too meek and should behave with more firmness, we had to admit that he appeared content with his lot.

It came as a shock, therefore, when Peggy wrote that she had left Bill and was going to sue for divorce on the grounds of cruelty.

Mother was horrified. We never did get to the bottom of it, but apparently everything had been triggered off when Peggy became friendly with a bookmaker - rather too friendly for Bill's liking. He had already received several anonymous letters (alleging her wayward behaviour) but had sensibly burnt them. One evening, however, Peggy returned home after midnight, flushed and excited. When Bill asked if she had enjoyed herself, she told him bluntly that she had never had so much fun, and it made her realize what a fool she had been all these years.

Something must have snapped in Bill's brain, and he struck her hard across her face so that she fell heavily and awkwardly, injuring her back on the arm of a chair. She left him a week later.

As soon as possible after the divorce, Peggy married her bookmaker and they moved to Scotland. We heard nothing more from her, but I think Bill heard bits of news via his sons.

Bill did not re-marry, but to our surprise, he got over Peggy quickly and, within a year, became the smartly dressed man of thirty years earlier. His clothes were immaculate, and he looked prosperous. Promotion meant he was now Area Sales Manager, dealing in car spares, and he had moved to a bachelor flat on the south coast. We gathered he led a busy social life and we saw him infrequently. When we did, we were delighted to see how well and happy he looked.

On one of his visits to Mother shortly after Dad's death

in 1965, he ran into Lily's younger sister, Rose. She told him that Lily's marriage had been somewhat stormy, but she thought they had come to terms with themselves.

Would Bill and Lily have been happy had they married each other? We'll never know, but I have an odd feeling they might have done rather well together.

Frank, aged 14, when he won the scholarship to Lawrence's College, Birmingham

Frank

When Frank was about eighteen (1931 or 1932), he met a young sixteen-year-old beauty who had just returned from Australia. She was tiny and wore her long brown hair in 'earphones'. Her father was a farmer who had taken his family to Australia in the late 1920s to make a better life for them. Unfortunately, the Depression hit Australia as well and, before he lost quite everything, he decided to return to Britain. He had just sufficient money left to have a bungalow built, and then had to take whatever job he could get.

They had been in Australia exactly four years, and a lesser man might have cracked over the loss of all his money. Mr Aspley was made of stronger stuff. Dad had known him for many years and said he was a real character. A good farmer he may have been, but there was no hope for him on the land – certainly not at that time – so he got a job with the local council and set to work making the best of it.

Vola (who had been christened Viola), was the eldest daughter and she had two sisters – Margaret and Jessica. All were extremely good-looking, but Vola was a real beauty, and it was not just skin deep. She had a gentle, if shy, nature.

Frank did not have it all his own way, for there was plenty of competition for a smile from the lovely newcomer to the social life of Tamworth and district. He may have seen her first, but there were other young men hard on his heels.

There was great entertainment at one of the winter dances

at the Village Hall in Elford, when it was noticed that Vola was sitting down, with Frank on one side of her and his old schoolfriend, Frank Woolton, on the other. Each seemed to be daring the other to ask her to dance, whilst Vola sat blushing prettily and gazing longingly at the dancers.

Just at that moment, Fred Flowers came into the room, took in the situation, at a glance, and marched up to Vola. Before either of the Franks realized what had happened, she was foxtrotting away from them. This seemed to bring them to their senses and from then onwards, Vola danced every dance – with my brother somehow contriving to dance the last waltz with her.

Except when she was going to a dance, Vola was not allowed to be out after nine-thirty p.m. Her father was strict on this point and, seven years later, at their wedding reception, he told of one evening when Frank and Vola arrived home at nine-forty p.m. He had been pacing up and down the garden path and was in a fine old temper by the time they came into sight.

'What the devil do you mean bringing my daughter home at this time of night?' he stormed, while, at the same time, pushing Vola through the gate.

Frank was contrite. 'I'm sorry, sir, my watch stopped.'

'That's no excuse and if I find you hanging around here again, I'll put my foot behind you. My girl's a respectable girl and I'm not having her out until all hours.'

'But Dad—' began Vola.

'That's enough.' Mr Aspley pushed her into the house before him and slammed the door.

Once in the hall, he asked. 'Who is that young blighter anyway?'

When Vola told him, he blustered. 'Why the devil didn't you tell me?'

Vola silenced him with a quiet, 'You didn't give me the chance.'

The next day, Mr Aspley, happening to meet Dad in Tamworth, stopped for a chat, and mentioned that he was by no means displeased that Vola and Frank appeared to be friends, as long as she was home in good time. Knowing nothing of the previous night's encounter, Dad did not pass this onto Frank, who continued to date Vola, but left her a few doors away from her home and waited only to see her safely home before going home himself.

When Frank was nineteen, we left Elford and, for about a year, lived in a suburb of Birmingham as Mother had a notion to 'go into business'. Frank ran the small shop, but his heart wasn't really in it, and we went to live in Tamworth where we were all much happier. All the time we were away, Vola and Frank had kept up a spasmodic correspondence although Vola had plenty of escorts during those twelve, or so, months.

Within a few weeks of our settling in Tamworth, Frank brought Vola to tea one Saturday. Such excitement there was on the day as I helped Mother make the 'little extras' the occasion demanded. Frank had never before brought home a girlfriend and, indeed, had never shown lasting interest in anyone but Vola. It helped that we already knew her, and Dad knew her father so well.

From that day, we all knew that this was the real thing, as far as they were concerned, and it transpired that Frank was the only young man Vola ever introduced to her parents.

Of course, they had their ups and downs – such as the occasion Vola described to me many years later:

Frank was working in Birmingham at the time, commuting from Tamworth each day. Vola worked in a shop in Tamworth and normally the one night they did not see each other was on a Tuesday. They were not actually engaged at this time but there was, I suppose, an 'understanding'. Anyway, it appears that Fred Flowers had gone into the shop one Tuesday and, learning she would not be seeing Frank that night, invited her to go to the Pictures with him. It was a film Vola particularly wanted to see so she agreed. Unfortunately for her, Frank had business which brought him back to Tamworth earlier than usual that day, so he decided to give his girlfriend a nice surprise and meet her from work. When she came out of the shop, she was surprised alright, and glanced across to the Town Hall.

Frank followed her gaze and saw a mystified Fred Flowers, gazing at them. 'What's he doing there?'

Vola blushed.

'Is he waiting for you?'

'Well...er...'

'Then you can go across and tell him it's me you're going out with tonight, not him.'

'Oh, I don't—'

'Now look here, if you don't, I will. Only I won't say it as nicely as you!'

Vola went.

She told me that, in later years, she and Frank often laughed about it, but, at the time, she was furious with him. Soon after that, they were formally engaged.

It was indirectly through Vola that Bill met Peggy, who worked in the same shop (Woolworth's), though only briefly.

One Saturday night, Vola had been delayed and asked Peggy if she would explain to Frank that she would be a few minutes late. Bill, who was 'between girlfriends' at the time, was standing talking to Frank who introduced them. The attraction was immediate, although it was not until a fortnight later that Bill contrived to meet Peggy again, mainly because he had no help from Frank, who did not think much of Peggy.

As it turned out, Bill and Peggy, after a whirlwind romance, were married within the year, but Frank never really liked her. For some reason, she seemed jealous of Vola.

Vola, on the other hand, remained serene and gentle. She could stand up for herself should the need arise, but it hardly ever did because she was one of those happy people who can command respect just by being their natural selves. If she had any enemies, they would be people who envied her disposition. She produced a daughter of the same nature and a son who took after Frank. These two were a great comfort to her when my brother died suddenly at the early age of fifty-seven.

EDITOR'S NOTE

This is where Doris's written accounts of her early life end. Pretty much everything she told me over the years is contained within them. That is not to say they provide a definitive account of her life between 1920 and the early 1930s. But Mum preferred to remember the good times, in the main; the long sunny days before the world went mad in 1939.

EDITOR'S AFTERWORD

At two a.m. on March 13th, 2018, an old lady passed away in a side ward of Aintree Hospital near Liverpool, her only child by her side. Her passing was peaceful. Just the way she always wanted it to be.

When she was born, King George V was on the throne, worrying about whether his wife, Queen Mary, was intending to raise her hemlines above her ankles, and about the increasingly improper behaviour of his wayward eldest son, the future Edward VIII. Only women aged over thirty who fulfilled property owning criteria were eligible to vote and that right had only been in place two years. Mum would be eight years old before women finally earned the same voting rights as men. She was born into a world where everyone 'knew their place' and, with exceptions, tended to stick to it. The end of the Second World War would hasten social change in that regard, as in many others.

Much against her father's wishes, Doris volunteered for service and joined the Auxiliary Territorial Service (A.T.S.) and served throughout the war, achieving the rank of Staff Sergeant. She was responsible for administration relating to the posting of army personnel and others right the way through to 1945. She wrote of these years too but that, as they say, is another story.

Mum married in 1949 and, in keeping with tradition, took her husband's surname – Williams – by which she was known for the rest of her life. They had one child (me). My decision to revert my mother to her maiden name was a simple one. She may have been a 'Williams' by marriage, but she was a 'Buttery' to her core. Her parents were straightforward Shropshire country folk who hailed from the village of Tibberton near Newport, around forty miles from Elford. They had both been in service in the same grand house. Grandma was a nursery nurse and Grandpa a coachman and, later, chauffeur for the family. In the First World War, Jack Buttery served in the Shropshire Light Infantry where his driving skills were put to good use driving trucks in France. He spent the war years in some of the worst affected areas but spoke little of his experiences. I have learned this is in keeping with many, many others who have seen things no one should ever have to witness.

Of her two parents, Mum was closest to her father, although she loved her mother dearly. In temperament she had elements of both in her nature, but her kindness, compassion and sense of fair play came from both sides of her family. Looking back over her life many years later, she told me they didn't have much in the way of possessions, but life was somehow easier then and she counted herself fortunate to have had a happy and enriched childhood. The culture of consumerism was one she never aspired to during her life and even when she could have afforded to replace an old-fashioned piece of furniture or carpet, she would refuse on the grounds that it still had 'plenty of wear' in it.

She never forgot the lessons of 'waste not, want not', instilled in her since her earliest years. String would be carefully rewound for future use, as would undamaged gift paper. Christmas cards would be cut up for use as shopping lists or colourful gift tags. Scraps of cloth, left over from the days when she made clothes for herself and me, were carefully folded and stored in a drawer, where they remained until I turned out her house in 2018.

Mum's love of cats remained with her throughout her life, and she passed it on to me. I happily continue her legacy of 'knowing my place' – at least where felines are concerned.

Doris Buttery was a true product of her age and upbringing. That's not to say she couldn't adapt to changing times because she undoubtedly did, but she never lost sight of who she was and where she had come from. In keeping with her Buttery (and Hinks) heritage, she would always be a true friend to anyone who needed her.

I am proud and privileged to be her daughter.

Ann Nibbs
Southport, 2021

ACKNOWLEDGEMENTS

I am indebted to Greg Watkins who tirelessly pored through reams of documents on the trail of discovering who lay behind the pseudonyms, and who provided much-needed documentary clarification and confirmation of certain facts and dates. Thank you to Greg also for a fascinating guided tour of the village in June 2021. A truly memorable experience that brought me even closer to Mum's world as she knew it.

Thank you to the people of Elford, some of whom I have had the pleasure of interacting with on Facebook and elsewhere, and who have shared family memories with me.

Thanks also to Margaret Clarke of Tamworth Heritage Trust for her support and information. A visit to the Heritage Hub is well worth it. www.tamworthheritagetrust.co.uk/heritage-hub

I must also say a big 'thank you' to my intrepid husband, Colin Nibbs, who risked life and limb to take present-day photographs of the approach to Elford. This involved him standing in the middle of the road at the mercy of oncoming traffic. Fortunately, there wasn't any at the time. Maybe Mum was watching over him!

Elford, 2021
Ann Nibbs

If you are reading this and are unfamiliar with Elford, it is well worth a visit. It is a delightful village, much-loved by its inhabitants who maintain it so well. There is a strong sense of community which Mum would recognize, even if the houses are somewhat smarter than in her day. The cottage where she was born and grew up remains and has been extended in keeping with modern needs, and the walks she describes are still possible, with sustenance being served at *The Crown*, in the centre of Elford and *The White Lion* in Harlaston as it was when she was a girl.

Although long missing its great Hall, Elford Hall Gardens have been taken over by local volunteers and provide a peaceful haven from the hustle and bustle of the world: elfordhallgarden.org

St Peter's Church is much as Mum would remember it. There you will find the font with its magnificent steeple-like cover. The monuments and tablets to the Howard and Paget families are here too, along with a rather splendid brass plaque commemorating a certain William Williams who wielded his censer a little too enthusiastically in my grandmother's direction one Sunday: measevalleychurches.com/our-churches/st-peters-church-elford

In the churchyard you will find gravestones with familiar names including Charlotte Hodgett – formerly

Howard. You will also find some quite extraordinary trees. I'll leave you to discover them.

The school is much enlarged and now known as Howard Primary School, and the current Village Hall was erected and officially opened in 2008 – the one Mum knew having been demolished owing to its dilapidated state and the need for larger premises. Its successor has been tastefully constructed so that it is aesthetically in keeping both with the village and its predecessor.

For more information on the village and its landmarks, visit Elford Parish Council's website: www.elfordparish.co.uk

Approaching Elford, June 2021

The Crown, Elford June, 2021

The new Village Hall, Elford, June 2021

St Peter's Church, Elford, June 2021

Doris on her 90th Birthday, with daughter, Ann, and (Ann's husband) Colin Nibbs, October 23rd 2010